THE **MINDFUL** COUPLE

52 Weekly Strategies
to Real Love and Connection

THE **MINDFUL** COUPLE

CRAIG & DEBBIE LAMBERT

HAWK PRESS

ISBN 978-1-7333133-0-8 (paperback)
ISBN 978-1-7333133-1-5 (ebook)

Published by Hawk Press

Cover design by LJ Lafleur
Interior design by Fiona Lee

craiglamberttherapy.com

To Faith Lambert (Craig's mother)
and Abe Perel (Debbie's father)

CONTENTS

PART II
MANAGING CONFLICT

PART III
KINDLING INTIMACY, SEX, AND ROMANCE

INTRODUCTION: MORE CONNECTION, MORE LOVE, MORE JOY

IF you picked up this book, chances are you're in need of some simple tools to feel more connected, more loving, and more joyful in your relationship. As couples therapists, our biggest challenge is that couples wait too long to come for help. They struggle, fight, and get into a place where they feel hopeless and very triggered. By the time they get to our office, problems are festering in every area of the relationship. Why does this happen? When they get stuck, most people simply don't see and understand the dynamics, and they lack the skills to shift to a more loving place.

Here is the problem: we are not born with the relationship skills that we need. These must be learned and practiced, just like a new language or a new musical instrument. A solid relationship doesn't just happen. Cultivating one has to be a mindful and intentional practice. The good news is that there are skills that can truly transform relationships.

Over the past decade we have taught these skills to thousands of couples in private therapy and group workshops. The results are truly astonishing. We see couples come in disconnected and angry and leave hopeful, inspired, and often more connected than when they first met.

We feel blessed to have helped so many clients over the years and have a strong passion to share these tools with you. Our recommendation is that you approach them with a spirit of joy and play, for that is the energy that heals relationships.

To help guide you on your journey, we divided this book into three parts—Mastering Communication; Managing Conflict; and Kindling Intimacy, Sex, and Romance.

MASTERING COMMUNICATION

Most couples who come into our office say that they need better communication skills, yet the most important skills we need in relationships are never taught at home or at school. Fortunately, these skills can be easily learned and, when practiced, can heal, transform, and enhance all our relationships. When we master how to communicate with others, we become better partners, parents, employees, bosses, friends, and family members. We learn how to create connection when there's a division and, most importantly, we learn how to be present and open a sacred space between two human beings. Mastering communication is foundational to all of the tips provided in this book and so we begin here.

One of the most beautiful things about love relationships is that when we focus on creating a great relationship, we simultaneously embark on a journey of personal development. To create and maintain a great relationship requires us to stretch into new behaviors and open our hearts to another. Our relationships help us see how self-absorbed we can be. When we recognize that our partner has her own needs and desires, we can transcend our personal ego and care for and love another human being. This generally happens gradually, and these tips are designed to assist you on this journey.

Another important and often overlooked factor in our relationships is that we generally do not show up alone. We are children to our parents, parents to our children, sisters and brothers to our siblings, and we have friends and relatives. All of these relationships can create unanticipated stress and friction between partners. Different values, styles, and preferences, many derived from our early childhood programming, drive this stress and frustration. Being on the same page and communicating about these issues is not only vital to your relationship, it can also be quite healing.

MANAGING CONFLICT

Conflict is an inherent part of being in any relationship, yet when we experience conflict in our love relationships, it's particularly threatening. We long for connection and, unfortunately, conflict often creates separation. This separation feels threatening and lonely, and it often makes us sad, scared, frustrated, and angry.

Here's the good news: experiencing conflict as a couple can ultimately bring you closer. We know, it sounds counterintuitive, but at the heart of every conflict is the seed of our desire and unmet needs. Uncovering and communicating those needs and desires is the foundation of a healthy, loving relationship. These tips help you get below the surface complaint and uncover what's truly going on. At this level, connection can be reestablished and love can grow.

KINDLING INTIMACY, SEX, AND ROMANCE

When we first start dating, intimacy, sex, and romance are usually in full force. Oxytocin is running like crazy through our bodies, so we are on a true hormonal high and neither partner can do wrong. Everything is perfect... until it's not. How do we maintain or bring back intimacy, sex, and romance in our lives after the initial romance has passed? Over the years, we gain shared experiences, perhaps kids, and memories, and we often lose what brought us together in the first place. We long to go back to that magical time. These tips are designed to help you navigate your way back to a different but often richer starting place.

OUR INTENTION IS to provide you with fifty-two of the foundational tips we give our clients—one tip for each week of the year. Feel free to choose tips not necessarily in the order they're presented (although you could read them that way, too) but according to what you need to learn or what would be most nourishing to focus on for a given week. Each tip includes a "practice" for you. *We don't learn by knowing; we learn by doing.* The practices are short, simple, and easy to implement. We encourage you to read the tips and, most importantly, do the practices together.

A note about the language in this book: We work with all kinds of couples and see similar issues coming up, regardless of gender compositions. We've chosen to use masculine and feminine pronouns interchangeably, knowing that most, if not all, of the issues we describe could apply to anyone.

It is with great love that we offer you these simple yet highly transformative tips and practices.

Above all, have fun and play!

CRAIG AND DEBBIE

PART I

Mastering Communication

I

LEARN HOW TO EMPATHIZE

"No one cares how much you know,
until they know how much you care."

Theodore Roosevelt

DEBBIE had a ten-year-old client who once said to her, "When I get sad, my mom makes me angry."

Debbie asked what her client's mom did to make her angry. The little girl said, "My mom's always doing things and trying to help me, but I just want her to be there with my sadness. I want her to be sad with me... that's all." This little girl had a strong need for empathy and her mom only knew how to help by trying to fix something. We see this in relationships all the time.

Trying to fix is a well-intentioned gesture. The only problem is that it doesn't help. When empathy is needed, only empathy will work. In our relationships, why do we often go into fixing mode rather than empathizing? Probably because we don't know how to empathize and so we fall back on the tools that we're most comfortable with.

So how does one empathize? First, by understanding what empathy is. Empathizing in your relationship is imagining and, to some extent, experiencing the same emotions that your partner is going through. It is the ability to truly see, understand, and connect with your partner's feelings. Empathy creates kindness, compassion, safety, vulnerability, and a type of connection that can be very healing to your partner and to the relationship.

PRACTICE FEELING IT

The language of feelings may not be familiar to you. The exercise "Identify Your Feelings" at the end of this book provides a comprehensive list of feelings that might aid empathetic conversations about emotions. Also, we highly recommend you view the video "Brené Brown on Empathy" on YouTube (see the Sources and Resources section). Then, try the following:

1. Ask your partner to tell you about something that's creating fear, anger, frustration, resentment, guilt, sadness, or hurt.
2. As your partner shares, listen carefully and try to uncover the underlying, upsetting emotions. Pay attention to your partner's facial expressions as well. After your partner finishes speaking, see if you can identify what your partner is feeling. Try phrases like, "Given what you are saying about... I imagine you may be feeling... Is that what you are feeling?"

3. If your partner says, "Yes," you may say something like, "That must be very hard."
4. If your partner says, "No," then ask, "Can you tell me how you are feeling?" and repeat back what your partner says.
5. Switch roles.
6. Once you've both taken turns empathizing and being empathized with, discuss two questions:
   - How did it feel to be empathetic?
   - How did it feel to receive an empathetic response from your partner?

2

COMMUNICATE LOVE NONVERBALLY

"The beauty of a woman must be seen from in her eyes, because that is the doorway to her heart, the place where love resides."

Audrey Hepburn

NONVERBAL communication is always happening, with our tone of voice, facial expressions, touch, eye contact, and so on. Our partners will usually detect—and believe—unspoken communication, since it's difficult to conceal nonverbally what we are feeling. People watch what we do more than what we say.

Eye contact is particularly important when communicating with your partner. It can provide important emotional information. Perhaps without consciously doing so, we search each other's eyes for signs of a positive or negative mood—

and in many cases the meeting of eyes arouses strong emotions. It's easy to know when someone is tired, afraid, angry, happy, interested, sad, or frustrated by looking into her eyes. The better we get at reading our partner's facial expressions, the more aware and connected we become.

One day, Debbie pointed out that Craig's facial expression looked angry or mean. Craig decided to be more mindful and consciously soften and warm up his eyes whenever speaking to Debbie. He asked her for feedback and she said his gaze looked more loving—and, more importantly, she felt more loving towards him.

Tone of voice is another powerful way we unconsciously communicate our feelings. Debbie's dad would often raise his voice when he was angry. Debbie's mom would say, "Abe, stop yelling!" And he would reply, "I'm not yelling! I'm just talking loud!" What we think we are doing can often be very different from how we are perceived, particularly if we learned our style growing up. Is your tone of voice something that conveys love or is it used to accentuate anger?

How often do you touch your partner just to say, "I love you, I see you, I am here for you"? Touch is a nonverbal way of communicating love and connection. Do you use touch to communicate love in your relationship? Could you do it more?

PRACTICE SAYING IT WITHOUT WORDS

Here are some fun practices to help bring more awareness to your nonverbal communication:

1. Practice creating a facial expression, particularly around your eyes. Make it soft, warm, and loving when you speak

to your partner. Do this throughout the next week, until it feels more natural, and then ask each other whether you noticed a difference.

2 Have fun practicing with your partner. Express an emotion (for example, sadness, joy, or confusion), using only your facial expressions while your partner guesses which feeling you're trying to communicate. If your partner guesses correctly, she gets one point. Then it's her turn to nonverbally express. Whoever gets to five points first wins. To step it up, use only your eyes and cover the rest of your face.

3 Play the "Really Game." Take turns saying the word "really." Tell each other what you hear in your tones of voice: Anger? Disdain? Surprise? Confusion? Disbelief? Joy? Curiosity? Then take turns saying "really," but now with the intention of communicating love. Give each other a rating from 1 to 5, assessing how much love you feel, with 1 being "not feeling it at all"; 3 being "feeling some love for sure"; and 5 being "OMG, that feels so good." Keep going to see if you can get to a 5. Play with changing your tone until you get there. Have fun with it and enjoy giving and receiving the feedback!

3

CREATE A RELATIONSHIP VISION

"If you don't know where you're going, you will wind up somewhere else."

Yogi Berra

WE are the creators of our own reality. Our ability to visualize a desired future is unique to being human and foundational to creating the life we want. Many of us intuitively understand that our brain interprets mental imagery as equivalent to real-life action. When we visualize our goals unfolding and feel the feelings, we are creating neural pathways that prime our mind and body to carry out actions consistent with what we imagine.

What would it be like if you and your partner decided to be together and you never discussed things like whether you want to have children together (and how many), how you express spiritual values, where you want to live, where and how often you want to travel, how you relate to money, and what you like to do for fun and to stay healthy? When we commit to being with someone, we assume that we're on the same page only to find out later that we are not. So often we have unspoken yet clear ideas of what we want for our future. Perhaps one partner visualizes retiring in a small rural community while the other envisions retirement by the beach. Or perhaps one values and expects to spend quality time with his partner throughout the week, while the other may think that's more appropriate for the weekends.

In our practice, we guide most couples through a visualization to create a mutual relationship vision. A relationship vision creates a roadmap for your lives together and gives direction to each decision and action that you make. The exercise is based on the idea that visualization and intention are the two most valuable skills for creating change. The visualization process helps couples identify and work towards their goals and experience their desired reality. Without a clear relationship vision, all of us are bound to run into difficulties.

PRACTICE CO-CREATING A RELATIONSHIP VISION

Write down the following categories: being together, love and intimacy, spirituality, work, finances, communication, friends and family, and health. Then try this:

1. Individually, imagine something from each of these categories that you would like to manifest in your relationship.

Write down one for each category, in the present tense, as if it were already happening. For example, "We spend time away with each other at least six times a year."

2. Take turns sharing one item at a time with your partner. Does your partner share your vision? If not, make a note and take some time later to discuss areas where you disagree. If your partner does share your vision, have fun discussing what it would look and feel like to manifest that vision.
3. To take this practice further, try "Co-creating a Relationship Vision" in the Exercises section of the book.

4

GET TOGETHER WEEKLY

"Lack of communication is the key to any successful relationship going wrong."

Pepa

LET'S face it. Our lives are very busy. They are filled with many activities and demands, and, as a result, we often fail to touch base with each other on important details and issues that arise. Over time, we begin to feel disconnected from each other. The very things that keep us apart—work, kids, working out, connecting with friends and family—are the very things that we need to communicate about. Missing conversations becomes the breeding ground for resentment and misunderstanding. Couples sometimes go weeks without ever discussing the daily activities in their lives and even more significant issues such as how they're doing with the relationship.

This tip is simply to schedule one hour a week for a relationship get-together, during which you connect and catch up. Each week, set aside sacred time to talk about your relationship and how it has been going over the last seven days. The weekly relationship get-together helps couples stay connected and on top of important issues, events, and appreciations. It is one of the most important activities in a healthy relationship and also one of the least implemented.

All we can say is, *try it!*

PRACTICE YOUR WEEKLY GET-TOGETHER

Try these suggestions for structuring your get-together:

1. Pick a time and place that feels relaxing and comfortable for both of you. If you have kids, perhaps schedule your time together for the evening, after bedtime, or on the weekends when the kids are doing an activity. Schedule a time when you're least likely to be interrupted.

2. Make it fun, if possible. Some of our couples choose to get together over a dinner out during the week. Sometimes we will start a meeting on a weekend hike and finish it at home when we are in front of our calendars. For some couples, having no distractions may make the meeting easier, so consider creating some quiet time at home. The point is, create a structure that works best for both of you and stick to it.

Here's a sample list of agenda items. For each time you get together, pick the items both of you feel are the most important to cover for that week. If you have enough time, consider including all these items:

1. APPRECIATIONS Give each other an appreciation. (See tip 11.)
2. HAPPY/CRAPPY Take turns offering one "happy" and one "crappy" of the week.
3. CALENDAR REVIEW With your calendars in front of you, review the upcoming week, reminding each other of appointments, chores, activities, or events.
4. WEEKLY DINNERS Discuss your work schedules so you both know what nights to expect each other home for dinner, and then plan dinners.
5. SOCIAL EVENTS Schedule weekly dates, vacations, family outings, get-togethers with friends.
6. STRESSORS Pick a stressor that you are currently facing and would like to discuss. It may be the "crappy" you shared or it could be something else. If it's an issue that may result in conflict, mirror each other along the way. (See "Mirroring" in the Exercises section of the book.) Never resist slowing down the conversation. Maybe say, "I think we should slow this conversation down a bit. I'm thinking that we should try mirroring each other."
7. DECISIONS Identify and resolve any outstanding decisions the two of you may need to make. If necessary, schedule a separate meeting to address these.

5

BUILD TRUST

"Trust is built in very small moments."

Brené Brown

WHAT is trust in a relationship? Most of us think of trust as being faithful, when actually it is so much more. Trust is a major value and central ingredient in intimate relationships. It means that your partner has your best interests in mind and would not do anything to intentionally hurt you. Trust is knowing that your partner will do the following:

- Be there for you when you reach out
- Be there for you when life gets messy
- Be there for you when you're not at your best
- Keep the promises that you make to each other

Trust manifests in many ways, but it usually has to do with certain needs being met consistently. If your partner is emotionally unavailable, critical, defensive, or rejecting, this will create mistrust, which usually results in the fear and belief that your relationship is not a safe place for you to be vulnerable. To feel safe and secure in our relationship, we need to know that we can trust our partner.

How much trust is there between you and your partner? How might you create more trust? For most of us, physical and emotional intimacy lays the foundation for building trust and security.

PRACTICE TRUST

Try these exercises to build trust with each other:

1. Set aside time to answer the following questions individually; then share your answers and discuss:
    - On a scale of 1 to 10, how would you rate the level of trust in your relationship?
    - What is one thing that you do that may erode your partner's trust in you?
    - What is one thing that your partner does that erodes your trust in him?
    - What is one thing you can personally do to increase trust?
    - What is one thing that your partner can do to increase trust?
    - What is one thing your partner does to help you feel secure and cared about?

2. Make a declaration to each other: "I know I have done things in the past to erode trust in the relationship, and I want you to know that I am committed to building your trust to a higher level. My promise moving forward is that I will . . ."

3. Play with touch. Since physical touch can also increase trust, play with at least one of the following "trust positions" that establish a sense of physical security and connection:

   - Sit up with your back supported while your partner lies down, with his head on your lap, and stroke his hair.
   - Lie down next to each other holding hands and talking.
   - Lie down with your chest against your partner's back, arms around him, and breathe in unison.

4. Do a trust walk. Have your partner close his eyes while you lead him around the neighborhood. Make sure he feels comfortable and safe. Then switch positions. Discuss your experiences both as leader and follower. Was it easier to lead or follow? Did the experience get easier or more difficult over time?

6

DE-STRESS THE HOLIDAYS

"The most important thing in communication is hearing what isn't said."

Peter Drucker

HOLIDAYS can be a challenging time of the year for couples and families because of the unintended stress that can accompany them. Sources of stress can include a lack of time to get things done, pressure to give gifts, the cost of gifts, workplace demands, and, of course, finding ways to celebrate with two sets of families. For some people who live far from family, it can be lonely as they miss seeing their loved ones at this time of year. During the holidays, difficult emotions may come up for those estranged from family, too. It's also common for people to feel emotional distance from those they're spending the holidays with, so they might feel lonely even in a room full of people.

Blended families create another challenge during the holidays. Trying to figure out where the kids will be and getting everyone together at the same time can create surprising amounts of stress and often disappointment. Tried-and-true family traditions may become stressful and obligatory over time without people even realizing it until the stress becomes too much.

A common cause of communication breakdown during these times of year is not addressing issues until after they arise, and, even then, they often get swept under the carpet because of the momentum of the holidays. In advance of the holidays, it's important for partners to talk honestly and openly with each other about their expectations, hopes, and fears.

PRACTICE STRATEGIZING FOR THE HOLIDAYS

Find a time before the holidays to sit down (perhaps in your weekly get-together; see tip 4) and strategize about how you'll manage the holidays together. Respond to the following questions separately and then have a dialogue to compare answers:

1. Which family traditions and rituals would you like to follow during the holidays?
2. What is one thing that is really important to you during the holidays, something that you feel you cannot compromise on?
3. Name one thing that can make you sad, disappointed, or frustrated around the holidays.

4. What possible problem areas may come up during holiday time, with each other or with other family members?
5. How would you like to handle problems?
6. What are some ideas for how your partner can support you?
7. Reflect on past experiences with your partner. Think about his frustrations, disappointments, needs, or expectations. What two things can you do for your partner that you think would really support him during the holidays? What needs can you fill that would delight your partner?

7

TREAD DELICATELY AROUND WEIGHT ISSUES

"It is difficult to make someone feel better about their body, but it is very easy to make them feel worse."

Lynn Saladino

IF you're thinking about mentioning your partner's weight, don't do it! Weight gain often occurs as we age—and as we become comfortable in our relationships. Unfortunately, many people have complained to us about their partner's weight gain, saying it factors in a loss of sexual interest in either him or her. American culture plays a key role in how people are attracted to each other. It says: "Thin is in." When we meet, most of us first experience physical attraction, which motivates us to dig further and learn more about the other person. It may be true that women care less about their partner's looks than men do, but women seem to be more sensitive about their own looks, especially about gaining weight.

It should be obvious that weight, especially for women, is among the most delicate of conversation topics. Everyone wants to hear "I love you no matter what." But what do you do if you've lost sexual interest in your partner because of weight gain? One problem with telling your partner that she's overweight is that she already knows, and she probably feels guilty and afraid of losing your love. She certainly doesn't need you to point it out. However, your partner might appreciate your help in tackling it with healthier lifestyle choices the two of you can make together.

If you are concerned that your partner has gained too much weight, the best advice we have for you is this: Do not share your observation under any circumstance. It's a no-win situation. Instead, think about what you can do to change your lifestyle habits as a couple. Weight aside, it's hard for one person in a partnership to make changes alone. Perhaps your lifestyle choices as a couple are contributing to your partner's weight gain, particularly if dates and social outings center on meals and drinks.

PRACTICE MAKING YOUR PARTNER FEEL GREAT

Here are some things you can do to help a partner who's gained weight:

- Buy her some great-fitting clothes—things she can wear out, with you, and feels fantastic in. Celebrate how she looks right now and she'll beam with confidence.

- Join a gym together, encourage your partner to join yours, or recommit to the gym membership you already have.
- Twice a week, trade "date night" for "workout" night. Take a Pilates, yoga, or salsa dance class together, or go on an evening bike ride.
- Tell your partner that you want to improve your diet—and you need her help to do it. Then, sign up for a cooking class that emphasizes healthy recipes and start cooking healthy meals together.
- If your partner complains about her weight, don't agree with her or deny it; just ask, "How can I help?"

8

MAKE REQUESTS—THEY GET YOU FURTHER THAN DEMANDS

Requests, by definition, can be refused; demands cannot.

ARE you confused about the difference between making a demand and making a request? It's easy to be unclear about this. Requests are received as demands when your partner believes he will be blamed or punished if he does not comply.

When your partner hears you make a demand, he sees only two options: submission or rebellion. Either way, the person making the demand is perceived as controlling, and the listener's capacity to respond openly to the request is diminished. Asking for what you want and need in a relationship is important, but it becomes a demand when the other person does not feel he has the right to say no without getting punished in some way.

The difference between a request and a demand is determined by how you treat your partner when he says no. You can help your partner trust that you are requesting, not demanding, by indicating that you would only want him to comply if he can do so willingly, even happily.

Here are two examples:

SARAH I am lonely and would like you to spend the evening watching a movie with me.

JACK No, I'm really tired.

SARAH You know how lonely I am feeling. If you really loved me, you'd stay up and watch a movie with me.

• • • • •

SARAH I'm very tired tonight. Would you mind doing the dishes?

JACK I'm wiped out, too. Let's do them tomorrow morning.

SARAH Okay, that sounds like a good idea.

Do you see the distinction between the two scripts? In the first example, Sarah guilt-trips Jack when he refuses her request, rendering it a demand. In the second example, she accepts his alternative to her genuine request. But note the difference in Jack's responses, as well. The first is simply a refusal. In the second example, Jack turns down Sarah's request but points to another possibility (doing the dishes in the morning). Coming up with another alternative is also a request, one for compromise. When you cannot fulfill a request, a healthy no is one that points to other possibilities.

PRACTICE NO-STRINGS REQUESTS

This week, each of you make a request of your partner, with the understanding that you are giving each other complete freedom to say yes or no. Keep these two points in mind:

1. When making a request, be as specific and loving as possible with it. Your goal is to make sure it is truly a request and not a demand. And remember, there can be no strings attached.
2. When responding to a request, if your answer to the request is a no, consider coming up with an alternative. "I don't have time to go to the movies tonight, but I do Wednesday night. Would that work?"

9

LIFESTYLE CHANGE—GO IT ALONE, SOMETIMES

"And ever has it been known that love knows not its own depth until the hour of separation."

Kahlil Gibran

A LIFESTYLE change is any situation involving a journey of self-improvement, such as eating healthier, exercising more, going back to school, quitting alcohol, and so on. Sometimes a lifestyle change involves one partner quitting an activity that both previously enjoyed. We see this often with drinking. It's particularly difficult when, in the past, drinking has been a mutually satisfying activity that created a bond. The partner who doesn't want to lose a drinking companion often feels angry and resentful and has a hard time supporting the decision.

What happens if only one partner wants to make a lifestyle change? Although we believe it's always best for partners to do major lifestyle changes together, this isn't always possible. Our advice when it comes to lifestyle changes is that it's always better go it alone than to insist your partner participate. That's a common mistake we see.

Craig is a real yoga person. He goes to classes four times a week and on numerous weekend retreats throughout the year. He'd like it if Debbie shared his passion for yoga, but it's certainly not a deal breaker. And while Craig says, "Who knows? Eventually she may want to join," Debbie consistently says, "Probably not." She appreciates Craig's flexibility about her not joining him. She is just not yoga girl.

Pressuring your partner into something she doesn't want to do just lays the foundation for resentment and unnecessary conflict. Your change is for you, so respect your partner's right to make her own choices. The less resistance that's created, the more love and support are allowed to enter. When we support our partners in lifestyle changes they desire, they feel loved and respected and, as a result, more loving and connected in the relationship.

PRACTICE SUPPORTING CHANGE

Think about a lifestyle change that one of you has made or plans to make, and then practice supporting that change by taking these steps:

1. Discuss when and why the change is being made. If you've already made the change, revisit the reasons for it.
2. Give the person who's not initiating this lifestyle change time to adjust to the idea and understand the reasons for it.

3. If there is resistance to the change, explore it. For example, the person who's not changing may be angry because it means his partner will be less available, or he may be insecure about the new people his partner will be involved with.
4. Request specific kinds of support from your partner. For example: "Can you prepare meals for the kids on the nights that I go to the gym? That would help me to not feel pressured to run home and cut my workout short."

10

LEARN YOUR LOVE LANGUAGES

"We cannot rely on our native tongue if our spouse does not understand it. If we want them to feel the love we are trying to communicate, we must express it in his or her primary love language."

Gary Chapman

GARY Chapman is arguably the country's most successful marriage therapist. His book *The 5 Love Languages* has been on the *New York Times* bestseller list for eight straight years. His main advice, as obvious as it sounds, is to figure out what specifically makes your partner feel loved. In other words, what is her love language? According to Chapman, it's probably one of five things:

1. Affirming words
2. Quality time
3. Acts of service
4. Physical touch
5. Receiving gifts

The most common mistake we make in relationships is to speak our love language and assume that our partner speaks the same one. For example, in Craig and Debbie's relationship, Craig's primary love language is affirming words. Debbie's is acts of service, followed by receiving gifts. It would be a mistake for Craig to offer affirming words to Debbie and believe that they will fill her the same way they do him.

Everyone feels loved in different ways. Loving behaviors can range from your partner bringing you a cup of coffee before you get out of bed in the morning to the two of you setting aside some uninterrupted "us time" every other weekend for home-repair projects. One person may want a back rub and the other an occasional date night out on the town.

So how are we supposed to know what makes our partner feel loved? It's actually quite easy: we ask. This prevents mind reading and avoids potential disappointment.

PRACTICE EACH OTHER'S LOVE LANGUAGES

To learn your love language, take Gary Chapman's 5 Love Languages® Quiz for free at 5lovelanguages.com. Then try this:

1. Individually, write down five to ten specific things that are meaningful to you and that would make you feel loved.
2. When you've completed your lists, read them to each other.
3. Exchange lists and, based on the items, guess what your partner's love language is.

4. Review your partner's list and circle all items you are willing to do.
5. Choose at least one behavior from the list and start doing it. If it helps (and it usually does), schedule a reminder in your calendar.
6. When your partner does a loving act for you, acknowledge it with an appreciative comment. So often we hear that our clients have stretched into new behaviors only to go without acknowledgment for them.
7. Add behaviors to your list as they occur to you and share them with your partner.

II

RITUALIZE APPRECIATION

"Appreciation is a wonderful thing: It makes what is excellent in others belong to us as well."

Voltaire

NOT being appreciated is one of the top complaints we hear in therapy. "She just doesn't appreciate anything I do" or "I can't do anything right" are common criticisms from both partners. How is it that we lose our capacity to appreciate what we like over time and instead see what annoys us so much clearer? Why do we fail to give our partners what we want ourselves (appreciations) and instead give them what we don't want (complaints)? The primary reason is that what we first appreciate and find amazing about our partners becomes just the standard over time. Maybe when you met your partner, he was always on time and your previous partner had always been late. You were overjoyed in the beginning, but after ten years, although you appreciate it, you may feel odd even mentioning it.

When we're not acknowledged for the wonderful things we do, even if these things come naturally to us, we become burnt out and feel... well... unappreciated. This can lead to a lot of dysfunction, such as the following behaviors:

- Getting into arguments over the little things
- Being more emotional
- Being quieter, more distant
- Not asking for our partner's opinions
- Making plans without consulting the other
- Not being as interested in romance
- Having an affair

Most of us are just as uncomfortable giving appreciations as we are receiving them. The good news is that, with a little practice, both giving and receiving appreciations can be as easily done and feel great.

Of course, the most common way to give appreciations is in the moment with a heartfelt thank-you: "I really appreciate you helping me... or doing that... or saying that..." and so on. However, it's not easy or practical to appreciate in the moment a lot of things that our partners do. That is why we suggest a morning ritual of giving appreciations.

PRACTICE APPRECIATION

Every day, scan your environment for things to appreciate about each other. An appreciation can be for something as simple as making the bed. Use the following script, adapted from the work of Harville Hendrix, to develop the habit of giving a daily appreciation. Do this at the same time every day: for example, before you get out of bed in the morning or when you get into bed at night. The ritual should only take five minutes. Here's the script:

SENDER (THE SPEAKER) One thing you did yesterday that
I appreciate is...
What makes that so special to me is...
And when you did that it made me feel...

RECEIVER (THE LISTENER) What I hear you saying is...
[Repeat what you just heard.]
What touched me about what you just shared is...

At the end of this dialogue, switch roles so that the sender becomes the receiver and vice versa. If you're thinking this sounds robotic, you're not alone. Almost all of our clients feel this way and nearly all of them benefit from this practice. So jump in and try it!

12

BALANCE "US TIME" AND "ME TIME"

"Let there be space in your togetherness."

Kahlil Gibran

WHILE loving conversations and "us time" are extremely important for couples, so is being respectful of your partner's need for space. In relation-ships, time apart is as important as time together. Couples need space in their relationship so they don't suffocate each other.

Not surprisingly, many couples find themselves in conflict over striking the right balance. A lot of people, such as Craig, for example, recharge their batteries with alone time. They enjoy solitude or sitting quietly and sometimes feel like they need it for their own sanity. Others are like Debbie, who recharges her batteries by being around and talking with people; interactions seem to nourish and replenish them. Either way, balancing time apart and time together is extremely healthy. It encourages both partners to maintain their own sense of identity.

Expressing the need for alone time or time together can make all the difference in the world. If you're the partner who needs more space, instead of saying, "Leave me alone!" try one of these approaches:

- "I love you, and I need time for myself right now."
- "I need a little quiet time so I can get some work done. Is now a good time?"
- "I want to spend time alone now, but could we spend time together after dinner?"

If you are the partner who needs more together time, either with just two of you or with others, consider saying:

- "I feel a need to spend more time with our friends. Can we plan something this week or next?"
- "I feel a need to spend time with the girls [or the boys]. Would you mind if I go out with them on Friday night?"
- "There is a party at Sue's house this weekend. Would you like to go? If not, would you mind if I go by myself?"

Another concern that comes up is taking alone time when you're in the same house or room. For example, it's very comforting for Craig to spend time with Debbie while they do separate activities. Sometimes, just being in each other's presence is enough. Debbie has learned how important Craig's quiet time is, and she uses it to get work done for herself. There's an advantage, too: since she can be a little distracted, it's helpful when Craig is working because it encourages her to focus.

When there is a clear understanding of each other's needs—whether it's for "us time" or "me time"—couples can relax into the space of together and apart.

PRACTICE THE BALANCE OF TOGETHER AND APART

Talk about your balance of time together and apart. Share what you appreciate about how it is now and brainstorm how to create more balance, if it's needed. You may have different ideas about this, so be sure to fully listen to what your partner needs. Think creatively to establish the desired balance for both parties. Here are some possibilities:

- Take turns having nights out so the other person can putter around the house.
- Agree to a code word for nights when you come home and just need to be quiet.
- Create separate office spaces within your home.
- Check in occasionally to make sure needs for alone time and together time are being met.
- Give each other quiet time to unwind after work.

13

COMPLIMENT YOUR PARTNER DAILY

"I can live for two months on a good compliment."

Mark Twain

WE all know how good it feels to receive compliments, yet most couples in our practice rarely give or get them. Our relationships can be lacking in compliments for many reasons. Often our parents rarely complimented each other and so it was never modeled for us growing up. Developing a habit of complimenting in this situation can feel awkward and unnecessary. "After all," you may think, "I didn't need compliments growing up... Or did I?"

While some of us find giving compliments difficult, receiving them can be challenging, too. We may dismiss a kind word by saying something like, "That's not true" or "You're just saying that because..." We may feel embarrassed accepting a compliment and so ignore it, and then, over time, our partner may stop giving us compliments.

How are you giving and receiving compliments? Do you look for ways to compliment your partner every day? How does it feel when you compliment your partner? Does it bring joy and a feeling of connection or is it more obligatory and routine? When you receive a compliment, can you let it land and really hear the words of appreciation, or do you feel more comfortable dodging or dismissing it? Can you smile and say thank you, even if you feel that the praise is unwarranted?

Giving and receiving compliments is a powerful communicator of love. Think about what would happen to the emotional climate of your relationship if both of you gave and received appreciative words daily.

PRACTICE DAILY COMPLIMENTS

Jump-start the process of love by showering your partner with compliments. Many of the couples we counsel have been moved to tears as they fill the space between each other with kind words. We learned this "Showering with Compliments" practice from Harville Hendrix. Here's how you do it:

1. Individually, write down ten or more things that you appreciate about your partner. You might start with physical features (for example, "I love your curvy figure," "I love your beautiful brown eyes," "I love your smile"); then move on to personality traits ("I love your confidence");

then do general qualities ("I love how hard you work to support our family," "I love it when you ask me about my day"). Always start your sentences with "I love." Work on this for about fifteen minutes.

2. Together, take turns "showering" each other with your compliments. Read slowly. Try to sustain the exercise for at least three minutes. End by telling your partner, with much enthusiasm, "I love you! I love you! I love you!"

3. Talk to your partner about how comfortable you are giving and receiving compliments. Rate your comfort giving compliments on a scale of 1 to 5 (with 1 being "very uncomfortable," and 5 being "very comfortable"). Choose a number for yourself and for your partner. Now share your ratings with each other and discuss. You may find that you agree on both ratings or that there are differences. If your ratings were 3 or under, discuss what you can do to help each other become more comfortable with giving compliments regularly. Next, do the same thing for receiving compliments.

Daily complimenting can produce intense feelings of love and connection, allowing you to experience something everyone yearns for, which is to be valued and appreciated.

14

COMPROMISING

A characteristic of a successful marriage is that each partner sincerely cares about the wishes and personal preferences of the other.

COUPLES constantly make decisions together. However, most couples we counsel have never really discussed how they make these decisions. Most couples consider the following subjects to be major topics that require discussion and agreement between them:

- Where to live
- How many children to have
- How to parent
- How to spend and save money
- How to divide household chores
- How much time to spend with extended family/in-laws
- When to take vacations and where to go

In the most successful relationships, partners are sincerely concerned about each other's wishes and personal preferences. Both are willing to go more than halfway to reach mutually satisfying compromises. Decisions and compromises are made willingly, instead of grudgingly. The happiest couples have the ability to negotiate; they openly share opinions and respect each other's points of view.

It's easy if you're on the same page. But when you strongly disagree or just can't find a compromise, you may quickly lose sight of the key ingredient that holds you together: the care that you have for each other. Anger, self-protection, and fear may take hold. Circling back to that love is the magic ingredient in difficult decisions—and the most challenging thing to do.

PRACTICE COMPROMISE

Try this:

1. Consider a current decision where you have differences of opinion and are struggling to come together, and do the following:

    - Individually, rate on a scale of 1 to 10 how willing you are to meet your partner's needs and truly make her happy. Give yourself a 10 if you can say, "Completely! I'm happy to compromise." (Hint: if you are struggling, you probably can't give yourself a 10.) Give yourself a 1 if the truth is "I refuse to compromise on this. I refuse to leave my position." Give yourself a 5 if your answer is "I will move off my position a little, but I can probably move more."

- If you've rated yourself a 5, 6, or 7, ask, "What can I do to push the number up to an 8?"

2. Consider some of the minor decisions you make as a couple that create repetitive struggles. One of ours is the decision to eat out or cook at home. Craig loves to cook at home while Debbie loves to go out. Recognizing this as a difference, we are very mindful to create a balance so both of us feel like we are getting our needs met. It's not tit for tat but rather a mindful consideration of the other's needs and preferences in the moment. What are some of the ongoing minor decisions you face?

Be generous in all of your decision making, and we guarantee that you will shift the energy and receive an equal amount of generosity from your partner.

15

UNDERSTAND THE ROOTS OF YOUR PARTNER'S ANGER

"Conflict is growth waiting to happen."

Harville Hendrix

FRUSTRATION and anger are a normal part of being in a relationship. Frustration is the result of things not going the way we want, and anger is the result of ongoing frustration. Most often, a persistent theme makes us frustrated and angry, and over time it just gets worse. We develop a story about what's happening (usually about how our partner is the contributor to our frustration) and then we react. This causes a less-than-desirable response in our partner (she takes it personally), and we begin the cycle of conflict. The worst part is that we rarely discuss what is going on. So how do we break this cycle?

When we work with couples who are experiencing ongoing conflict (and who isn't?), we often take them back to earlier childhood memories to discover the possible connection to present conflict. This allows both partners to see the dynamic more from empathy and love than from reactivity and ego. It opens up the conversation; the question becomes: "How can I help you heal this hurt and satisfy this need?"

Diving into possible causes of ongoing frustration and anger can be difficult for those of us who have done a good job suppressing them. Maybe your childhood was traumatic and one of your coping mechanisms was to suppress memories. Reaching back into the past with your partner and with the guidance of a therapist can be very healing but only if both partners feel comfortable. So proceed with caution and check in along the way to make sure you both feel safe and supported. The following exercises are relatively easy and can be quite powerful in provoking thoughtful and potentially healing conversations.

PRACTICE EXPLORING THE UNDERLYING NEEDS

The best way to explore the factors that cause ongoing frustration and anger for both partners is to identify an ongoing trigger, one for each of you. Maybe it is when your partner comes home late, or when your partner speaks to you in a patronizing voice or criticizes you for a particular behavior. If you are struggling to identify a trigger, ask your partner if she knows what triggers you. Once you have it, try the following:

1. Use the flowchart "Deconstructing Frustration and Anger" in the Exercises section at the end of the book and complete it individually.
2. Afterward, take turns being the speaker and the listener as you read each other your charts. The listener may mirror the speaker along the way or, at a minimum, summarize after step 7, step 8, and step 10. Note that step 10 is a request. Tell your partner whether you're willing to meet the request.

It can be very powerful to get in touch with root causes of anger. Explore with this list of prompts to get to the bottom of reactions:

- "What I mean by that is..."
- "An example of that is..."
- "My fear about this is..."
- "The story I tell myself is..."
- "And when you do that, I react by..."
- "And that usually results in..."
- "One thing you could do differently is..."
- "One thing I could do differently is..."

Set aside some quiet time when you can give each other undivided attention to respond to the prompts. It is an act of courage and love to fully open to your partner. Create a loving space.

16

DEAL WITH LIMITING BELIEFS ABOUT YOUR PARTNER

"The evidence doesn't support your belief. The evidence was created by your belief."

Abraham Hicks

We all have beliefs about our partners. Many are quite positive and some are . . . well, let's just say, *limiting*. We call these "limiting beliefs" because they diminish what we're able to see in our partner. If we have the limiting belief "My husband never listens," then all we pay attention to are the times when he doesn't listen. When he does listen, we don't notice or appreciate it.

In psychology, we call this "confirmation bias." We are programmed to look for things that confirm our worldview. Our brains are wired for this, and an associated adrenaline high comes from seeing the world according to our perspective. Confirmation bias explains why we've become so polarized with respect to politics—and why people become polarized in their relationships.

In relationships, confirmation bias looks like this: "He never listens to me" (limiting belief); "I observe him not having heard what I said" (evidence that confirms the belief); "I feel frustrated" (accompanying emotion); "I react by criticizing" (behavior). This criticizing results in your partner feeling he can never get it right.

In a way, he's correct.

So, how do we deal with the limiting beliefs we hold about our partner in a way that supports the relationship instead of harming it? How do we reprogram or let go of the beliefs that are there but no longer serve our relationship?

PRACTICE REPROGRAMMING

We can't change what we don't see, and this is especially true with limiting beliefs. Try this:

1. Individually, write down all the limiting beliefs you have about your partner. Hint: a limiting belief probably contains a universal qualifier (see tip 30), as in "He's *always* late" or "She *never* listens to me"; or it may be an overall assessment of personality: "She is selfish" or "He doesn't care about anybody but himself." Select a limiting belief you have about your partner that you would most like to work on.

2. Commit to catching your partner doing it right instead of wrong—and let him know you appreciate it when he gets it right. Be specific. For example: "I really appreciate you

showing up on time." Look for approximations of what you want. If your partner is normally thirty minutes late, recognize him when he's only fifteen minutes late.

3. Reframe conclusive limiting beliefs. Instead of saying that he's *always* late, choose a statement that's true and less conclusive: "He's late a lot and we just have different styles." Chances are, you're not going to change his behavior, so you're better off dealing with yourself when you get triggered by it! Find the positive, be compassionate, and even try to find some humor in the situation.
4. Decide to pick your battles. If it's not super-important, consider letting it go.

17

KNOW THE SECRET TO A GREAT RELATIONSHIP

"All that we are is a result of what we have thought."

Buddha

MOST of you are probably familiar with the documentary movie *The Secret.* It was a very popular film that focused on the law of attraction. We believe that the law of attraction is the single most important element in getting anything we want in life, whether it be success, health, happiness, or a great relationship.

The law of attraction simply states that anything we focus on, whether it is positive or negative, appears in our lives. This is profoundly important in relationships. Often, our knee-jerk reaction is to focus on the negative. We stew over the small stuff, it becomes bigger, and then we react. Our reaction produces a reaction in our partner, and we get more of what we don't want. We then get angrier and the cycle continues.

How do we change the cycle and use the law of attraction to attract what we do want? It's a simple answer but not always easy to implement. The answer is to focus on what we want, not what we don't want. This can be tricky, so let's look at an example.

"I want my partner to stop criticizing me whenever I forget something." Most people will focus on what they do not want; in this case it would be the criticism. But if you focus on "I really want him to stop criticizing me," you start waiting for him to criticize so you can "help" him by pointing it out... and we're off to the races!

Instead, we want to focus on "what I do want." It may be "I want my partner to be more supportive," "I want my partner to be more complimentary," "I want my partner to be accepting and understanding," and so on. By focusing on what "I want," it opens up new possibilities. We begin looking for times when our desires are met instead of catching our partner "doing it wrong." We become more open to having a conversation about what we want that is less triggered and more grounded in creating success, and, most importantly, we become less guarded and more compassionate.

The best way to create a great relationship by using the law of attraction is to seize opportunities to practice it in your daily life.

PRACTICE THE LAW OF ATTRACTION

Together, select a day to practice the law of attraction in your relationship. Consider posting a couple of reminders where you'll see them (in your car, at your desks, on the fridge). The notes could say, "Today, we focus *only* on what we want." During the day, try this:

1. Catch yourself in any negative thinking about what you don't want from your spouse. ("He doesn't make me a priority.")
2. Turn it around to focus on what you want. ("I want to enjoy my relationship and notice all the ways my partner shows that he's thinking of me.")
3. Attach an appropriate positive emotion to what you want. The emotion could be excitement, joy, or anticipation. *Feel* the emotion as you focus on what you want. ("When my partner is thinking of me, I feel joyful and connected.")

By concentrating on the last two steps—your positive thought and emotion—you're using the powerful law of attraction to draw what you want into your life, and you're on your way to whatever a great relationship is for you!

PART II

Managing Conflict

18

DON'T WAIT TOO LONG TO SEEK OUTSIDE HELP

The biggest problem with couples counseling is that couples wait until they are in stage 4—and there is no stage 5.

EVER wonder whether you and your partner need couples counseling? Here are some questions to consider:

- Have you lost interest in each other sexually? Does your relationship lack intimacy?
- Do you have difficulty discussing and deciding how to handle finances?
- Are either of you having a hard time forgiving and letting go of past hurts and disappointments?
- Are you having difficulty discussing and resolving differences?

- Are you or your partner unable to share feelings, listen to, and understand each other?
- Do you struggle with decisions regarding the division of responsibility, including household chores?
- Are you dissatisfied with the amount and quality of leisure time spent together?
- Are you dissatisfied with how your partner relates to your or her family and friends?
- Do either of you feel the other is too controlling or inflexible?
- Are you on the same page about how to parent your children?

Many of the couples who come to see us would answer yes to a lot of the questions above but have waited too long. Some have tried couples counseling before but didn't like the therapist or lost interest. Paying $150 or $250 a week might be a deterrent, and even if the fee is covered by insurance, the commitment to coming to the therapist's office weekly to talk about problems may be too daunting. Additionally, the lack of specific, measurable outcomes can leave couples wondering whether they are making progress at all. Couples can become frustrated with the slow, methodical process; they want a quick answer and resolution to problems that have been created over many years. Many get discouraged quite easily and then put counseling on hold until relationship concerns have metastasized to the point where problems are untreatable.

When you wait too long, issues that lie dormant, unresolved, or untreated sprout like cancer. Sometimes the symptoms are treatable and sometimes not: it depends on whether they have spread to other parts of the body, such as the heart, where the disease manifests as anger, frustration, emotional unavailability, loss of trust and respect. Or it could spread to the lungs, manifesting as unexpressed thoughts and feelings and as a sense of restriction and depression.

It's not easy to dismantle years of resentment and anger. So take our advice: if you feel that conflicts are mounting and negative feelings go unresolved, or if you lack confidence about the future of your relationship, then have a conversation about seeking couples counseling.

PRACTICE ASKING THE IMPORTANT QUESTIONS

Take some private time and honestly answer these questions together:

1. Do we want to improve this relationship?
2. What's our motivation for improving this relationship?
3. What might we need to change in this relationship for improvement to happen?
4. Are we both willing to work on these problems?
5. Is it time to seek outside help? If so, discuss:
    - What do we need to do to move forward?
    - What resistance may be present in seeking help?

19

TAKE RESPONSIBILITY INSTEAD OF BLAMING

"When you blame and criticize others, you are avoiding some truth about yourself."

Deepak Chopra

BLAMING is a close cousin of criticism and the energy is basically the same: "I am right; you are wrong. Now please fix it!" By the time couples come to therapy, they have refined the blame game into a fine art, with both partners feeling justified in their respective positions.

Feeling justified is easy, because we create a story about how wrong our partner is. The more we discuss the situation (that's putting it nicely—rarely does it feel like a discussion), the angrier both partners become. After all, it's very difficult to stay objective and even more so to take responsibility when someone is coming after you. When someone blames you, the normal response is to be defensive.

What's the solution? We encourage couples to nurture a climate of taking responsibility when things go wrong. Instead of jumping in with what your partner did to create or add to the undesired situation, think, "How could I have been a part of this situation?" Asking this question is the essence of taking responsibility. It is the foundation of emotional maturity but, unfortunately, not our knee-jerk response to breakdowns in our relationships. Here are some examples:

YOU SAY You let the car run out of gas and I asked you last week to fill it up.

TRY INSTEAD What can we do next time so that the car doesn't run out of gas?

• • • • •

YOU SAY You never listen; I don't feel heard.

TRY INSTEAD What can I do to make it easier to listen to me?

• • • • •

YOU SAY You're not giving me enough sex.

TRY INSTEAD I would love more sex, as you know. Is there something I can do or we can do to move more in that direction?

When we take responsibility, we are saying that it doesn't matter who is to blame. Blame is just a story, and the breakdown before us is our opportunity to learn, apologize, and plan to do it differently next time. Whenever anything goes wrong, it's an invitation to look at the lesson in it. One of our favorite quotes is from Marianne Williamson's *A Return to Love*: "The Holy Spirit has a highly individualized curriculum for everyone."

When we shift from blaming to taking responsibility, we move away from anger, frustration, and resentment and into the world of possibility, learning, and growth. When we take responsibility, we look for things we personally could do differently to prevent a repeat in the future, and this invites our partner to do the same.

PRACTICE CALLING IT

Make a pact that the next time you notice blame is happening, you'll call it. Say something like, "Are we playing the blame game again?" If the blamer calls it, he gets extra points, because it takes courage to call out ourselves. This is definitely the power move in a relationship and will go a long way in modeling the exact behavior you both want to see more of. Don't despair if your partner doesn't do the same right away. Keep up your end. Know that you're leading the way in creating a culture of taking responsibility. When we take responsibility, we are less concerned about what the other person is doing. Give your partner time. Build trust and over time she will come around.

20

FORGET FAIRNESS, TRY GENEROSITY

"For it is in giving that we receive."

Francis of Assisi

MARRIAGE or partnership, many believe, is a 50/50 proposition. That belief sounds good, and it seems to make sense. There's just one problem. It doesn't work. Here's why: Thinking our partner must do her "50 percent" leads us to focus on her performance. But once partners start measuring each other's performance, disappointment follows close behind, and a deadly cycle begins: "You're not doing your part" leads to unmet expectations, which leads to disappointment, then resentment and nagging, then increased pressure to perform, then disconnection instead of connection.

The problem with holding up fairness as a measuring stick for a good union is that it turns what should be a partnership into a contest. Scorekeeping is done unconsciously and there are no winners. Unfortunately, when you're constantly fighting for fairness, you never find fairness, and you only end up damaging the relationship.

So, what is the solution to this unhealthy cycle that we often find ourselves in? Instead of focusing on fairness, focus on generosity. Generosity means committing to giving our partners what they need without rendering a bill for service. Instead of saying, "I will come home earlier if you'll have more sex with me," we say, "I'll come home earlier because you need me to spend more time with you." This is a no-strings commitment to the welfare of our partners. There is a reciprocal exchange without anyone keeping score.

But, you may be thinking, what if one partner focuses on generosity and the other on fairness? How does that work over time? Not well! Shifting from fairness to generosity needs to be a mutual decision made for the sake of the relationship. Together, you must acknowledge that past behaviors may have been more self-focused and there needs to be a true desire to shift the energy from the self to the other. When each partner is focused on the other, magic happens!

PRACTICE THE GENEROSITY MIND-SET

It's not important whether one partner is more generous already. To shift to the generosity mind-set in your relationship, both partners need to acknowledge that being more generous will be healing and restorative to the relationship. Try this:

1. Together, ask if would it benefit your relationship if you *both* shifted from a mind-set of fairness to one of generosity.
2. Learn more about your partner's needs and wants. The tricky part is that these can change. Ask questions such as, "What can I do to help you right now?" or "What can I do to help you today?" Just the act of asking those questions is rooted in a generous mind-set.
3. If the answer is something that you feel some resistance to because of time or desire, try to stretch. If you can't stretch that much, then let your partner know that you want to support her and can't right now. Offer other more realistic options.

21

MAKE THE DREADED FINANCIAL CONVERSATION FUN

"I've always said money may buy you a fine dog, but only love can make it wag its tail."

Kinky Friedman

THE joining of two individuals is often the joining of two different orientations to money. Our early experiences shape our values about money, which operates metaphorically in our lives, representing many other things, such as the following:

- Security
- Power
- Intelligence
- Opportunity
- Trust
- The relationship between dependence and independence

It's little wonder that money is a major cause of conflict—and a multilayered problem—for many couples.

In our practice, couples often argue about money regardless of how much or how little they have. Deciding how to spend and how to save can be problematic. Some couples fight about money because they are struggling to make ends meet, and other couples fight about money because they can't agree on where to buy their fifth vacation home.

Where things break down is in a lack of communication and compromise. Whether you have $100 or $100,000 on the table to save or spend, the topic of finances requires thoughtful conversation and really listening to the needs and desires of your partner. Most people tend to avoid financial conversations like the plague, yet the only way to reduce conflict and move successfully towards what matters to both of you in life is to identify and reconcile differences.

Once we are on the same page, talking about finances can be a much more pleasant conversation. So, how do we begin?

PRACTICE MONEY TALK

Start with a conversation that uncovers some of the money-related issues that exist within each partner and between the two of you. Have fun with the following exercise, and feel free to make up some money questions of your own:

1. Individually, write down three things you appreciate about how your partner handles money. Share you answers.

2 Take turns answering the following questions:

- Name three things that represent what money means to you.
- What did you learn about money growing up?
- When do you tend to judge the ways others handle money?
- What are your three biggest fears about money right now?
- What's one thing you could do to lessen our conflict about money?
- What three things can we do as a couple to better manage our money?

These questions offer valuable insight into your approaches to money. They hack into your minds in a way that builds compassion and understanding between you. Once you understand each other, you can enter a more practical conversation that is filled with lightness and compromise.

22

PROVIDE SUPPORT, NOT SOLUTIONS

"An ear that listens can be medicine for a heart that hurts."

Steve Maraboli

IF you have been in a relationship for any length of time, you may have heard the words, "Don't try to fix it; I just need you to listen." When support is the only thing that's likely to help, trying to fix problems is guaranteed to create conflict. Listening, validating, and empathizing are foundational to healthy relationships, yet we all share a common drive to jump in with solutions. Sometimes, we don't want a "solution." We just want to vent, to have a sounding board so we can hear ourselves think, or just to have our feelings be understood and heard. When our partners jump in with solutions, we get frustrated and tell them they're not listening and their solutions are not helpful. Usually this only escalates. The solution provider gets a little defensive. "I am just trying to help you," he may shout, and the recipient only ends up feeling more frustrated and eventually hurt and angry as well.

When your partner just needs and wants you to listen, the most powerful thing you can do is mirror. Repeat back to her what she is saying. After all, she just wants to be heard and, by mirroring, you are clearly demonstrating that you are on the job. As you mirror, pay attention to how she receives you. Notice that she may say things like, "Exactly," "Yes, I know," "That's right..." These words tell you that you are on the right track. Lean in to it and enjoy giving her what she wants and needs.

PRACTICE LISTENING

Together, start by watching the informative video "It's Not About the Nail" on YouTube (see the Sources and Resources section for a link). This video by Jason Headley is probably the best we've seen that shows in a very comical but real way our tendency to jump to solutions and the frustration that is created for the person who just wants to be heard. The next time your partner solicits support, do the following:

1. Ask: "Do you need me to listen or would you like some suggestions and advice?" Nine times out of ten, she will say, "I just need you to listen." Believe her. Don't jump to solutions after you feel you've listened. Provide solutions only if she asks you for advice.
2. Empathize: Let her know that you know how she's feeling. For example, try saying, "It sounds like you are feeling

really frustrated!" Don't elaborate here. Just let her respond. Give her space to share how she's feeling, and be there for her. That is what she needs and wants.

3. Don't side with the enemy: If she says, "He's a jerk," don't say, "Well, maybe he is upset with you because of what happened last week..." Say instead, "I know. I can't believe he would do that to you." If she tells you her friend was twenty minutes late for lunch, don't say, "Well, maybe she had a good reason to be late. After all, you run late, too." Say instead, "I can't believe how inconsiderate that was."

23

LET GO OF YOUR STORIES

"Let go of your story so the universe can write a new one for you."

Marianne Williamson

MOST, if not all, of the couples we see have negative stories about each other that define the relationship. No matter how destructive it is, each partner hangs on relentlessly to the story and the associated feelings.

We hang on for many reasons. Among the most common is that we think if we let go or forgive our partner, we are letting her off the hook. We may feel that if we let it go, if we forgive, we are making what happened okay. We also hang on because we never really question the accuracy of our stories. We tend to believe they are true and that is basically the end of the story.

The truth is, there are many truths. When we hold on to a negative story, we are only grasping one truth. When the truth we cling to doesn't serve the relationship, it is generally time to find another story that is equally true *and* more supportive of the relationship.

For example, Craig and Debbie have a story about each other regarding politics. From the moment we met, it was clear that we were on opposite side of the political spectrum.

CRAIG'S STORY When I met Debbie, I thought she was naïve, clueless, and blinded by the rhetoric of her side.

DEBBIE'S STORY When I met Craig, I thought he was naïve, clueless, and blinded by the rhetoric of his side.

We have had many heated debates because, the truth is, we are blinded by what we choose to pay attention to. However, what we have learned to do instead is focus on where we have common ground. Now we choose to pay attention to how the other really cares about our country. We realize our values are quite aligned; we just disagree about how to get there. So, we focus on where we do agree and, most importantly, on how our care for each other is stronger and more important than anything else. Our disagreements have become just playful and academic rather than personal. Instead of creating stories about how we are different or better than the other, now we calibrate to our common ground and our love for each other.

PRACTICE KNOWING YOUR STORIES

Ask yourself, "What stories about my partner do I believe that keep me from being happy?" To discover your stories, think about a frustration you have with your partner. This may be something you discuss with your close friends or confidants. Once you've identified your story, try this:

1. Notice the thoughts that arise about the story and how they feel in your body.
2. Begin to imagine what it would feel like if you didn't believe this story. How does it feel to let go of it, even for one moment? What would be different in your relationship if you didn't believe the story?
3. What is another story, equally true, that you can use to replace your old story? Find a story that feels better and helps support a loving connection with your partner.

24

LOVE YOUR LOVER, NOT YOUR PHONE

These days, we give our phones more attention than we do our loved ones.

MANY people complain that time with their partners often gets disrupted by texts and emails. It appears technology is intruding on our romantic relationships. A study by Brandon McDaniel and Sarah Coyne, "Technoference," published in *Psychology of Popular Media Culture*, examines how technology interferes with relationships and concludes that cell phones are quite often damaging and disruptive to a relationship. High levels of "technoference" are associated with greater relationship conflict and lower relationship satisfaction.

When we attend to our phones instead of our partners, it feels to them like rejection—it hurts and they feel alone (unless they, too, are on their phone and then both partners are just disconnected, which is another problem). When a conversation, meal, or romantic moment is disrupted because of a text, email, or any other task, the message is, "What I'm doing on my phone is more important than you right now," "I'm more interested in my phone than in you," or, in some cases, "You're not worthy of my attention."

Rejections, even small ones, will cause resentment, a drop in mood and self-esteem, and eventually anger. If you think technoference might be causing problems in your relationship, work with your partner to address the issue. Talk to each other and assess the extent of the problem. Keep in mind that the demands of jobs or social/parenting obligations might necessitate exceptions to the rules.

PRACTICE INTERCEPTING TECHNOFERENCE

Craig and Debbie also struggle to keep technology from interfering with their relationship. Below you will find some ideas we personally have used or suggested to clients. These are the most successful ones!

- Establish tech-free zones. We created a tech-free bedroom and moved out all technology, including the TV, computers, Alexa, and our phones. It wasn't easy, at first, but we definitely noticed that we fell asleep quicker and slept longer after making these changes. It also got us out of the habit of watching the news before bed—not exactly the most romantic activity, especially since we are on opposite sides of the aisle politically! Now we read, talk, laugh, and... well, you know the rest!

- Make date night tech free. To avoid being tempted to check your emails and receive incoming calls, consider not taking your phone on a date night. If you must bring it, agree to set it aside completely when the meal comes.
- Have tech-free dinners. Both children and adults tend to hide behind their phones. Conversation is lost and the beautiful connection that was once part of the dinner ritual has disappeared. We tell our clients to place a phone basket near the dining room table and ask everyone to turn their phones off and leave them in the basket until dinner is over. It's so simple and we can't emphasize enough how transformative this can be.
- Make your car rides tech free. As we all know, it's illegal to drive and even touch your phone. But so many of us do. Not only is it dangerous, it is very rude to the passenger whose life you're putting in danger. As a passenger, it is equally rude to your driver to busily check emails and text messages. What do you expect your driver to do while you are busy being productive or entertained? Most importantly, you are missing a wonderful time to connect.

25

UNCOVER YOUR MONEY SCRIPTS

Money stories learned growing up can shape your financial life today.

CONVERSATIONS that help uncover long-held beliefs about money allow most couples to develop a better understanding of each other and ease conflict related to finances.

Debbie and Craig grew up with fathers who had a similar philosophy about money. The foundational belief was that old adage "Money doesn't grow on trees." Both our fathers deeply valued hard work and not wasting money. Ironically, both our moms also held similar values related to money, quite different from those of our fathers and more like, "Life is short, enjoy today..." Although we grew up with parents whose values closely mirrored one another's, our own values around money played out quite differently in our adult lives:

Craig is a saver and does not like to waste money. Debbie's attitude is more about living for the day without breaking the bank.

As you can guess, our differences play out quite vividly in our relationship. At first, these created a lot of conflict, with Craig trying to control things and Debbie trying to dodge any attempts at reining her in. It was only when we started talking about the messages we received during childhood that we were both able to create a healthier approach to our financial life together. We've been able to reframe the dynamic, each seeing the other's preferences (Craig's desire for control and Debbie's for freedom) as important needs to respect. We're no longer just fighting to get our individual needs met. As a result, today we have conversations that before would have certainly ended up in a serious breakdown.

PRACTICE GETTING THE MESSAGES

Schedule a time to talk about the money messages each of you received during childhood. Individually, answer the following questions and then share your answers:

1. What messages did you get from your father about money? What behaviors did you observe that supported those messages? How did you feel about his beliefs and actions around money?
2. What messages did you get from your mother about money? What behaviors did you observe that supported those messages? How did you feel about her beliefs and actions around money?

3. Did your parents fight about money? What specifically did they fight about?
4. In what ways did your parents agree about money?
5. During your childhood, did any outside events happen that could have affected your approach to money? (For example, a parent's divorce or loss of a job; the events of September 11, 2001; a recession or stock market crash.)
6. What is an important message about money that you want to hand down to your children?
7. Given your similarities and differences, what new stories and behaviors can you and your partner both adopt to create more connection around money?

26

SHOW UP ON TIME

If you are chronically late, you are chronically rude.

WE have all experienced making plans with people who are chronically late. When this happens with our partner, the result can be very disruptive, causing frustration, resentment, and anger. Believe it or not, Craig and Debbie have even seen this issue result in divorce.

If you are chronically late, you are asking your partner to chronically wait.

Debbie experienced this with a girlfriend years back. Debbie was chronically late by five to ten minutes. To Debbie, this was well within acceptable limits. Her friend, however, felt disrespected and resentful. She would say, "How can you make me wait so long!" Debbie's response was, "Why are you obsessing about this? Loosen up!"

Clearly, Debbie was defensive. But, one day, she really tried to understand why punctuality was so important to her friend. She finally realized that being chronically late legitimately disrespected her and her time: her friend had organized her day based on their agreement, and the time she spent waiting for Debbie was time she could have used for herself. Once Debbie realized this, changing her behavior was simple.

If you are a chronically late person, fess up and stop defending your behavior. Take responsibility. Remember, how you do anything, is how you do everything. If you are chronically late with your partner, chances are this same behavior shows up with many of your friends. Ask your partner exactly what the impact is on the relationship, and be prepared to listen without being defensive. Take notes and mirror what is being said (see "Mirroring" in the Exercises section). Really seek to understand.

For those who are chronically late due to disorganization, the internet is filled with strategies to help you. What we offer here is a mind-set tip. If you're chronically late because you're not thinking about the consequences for others, shift your thinking. With your actions, say, "I value your time. I honor our commitments fully. My word is central in our relationship, and you can trust what I say."

PRACTICE HONORING YOUR PARTNER'S TIME

Before your next time commitment with your partner, read the following:

1. Being on time is one of the ways I show the world, and myself, that I'm responsible.

2. My punctuality sends out a positive message about me to others. It is a reflection of how I show up in the world.

3. Today, I know that I can be on time for every commitment. It brings me great pride that others can depend on me to be on time.
4. I recognize that my life is better because I can be counted on to show up on time.
5. Being punctual is one way I show my respect to others.

27

BE CURIOUS ABOUT YOUR PARTNER'S PERSPECTIVE

"Out beyond ideas of rightdoing or wrongdoing, there is a field. I'll meet you there."

Rumi

FRIEDRICH Nietzsche, the great philosopher, teaches that there are no facts, only interpretations. When we're working with couples, oftentimes they have completely different perspectives on a shared experience. Why is this? We have a take on everything we observe, but it's not necessarily a fact. We interpret our world based on our own biases, judgments, and experiences. As the old saying goes, "We don't see things the way they are; we see things the way we are."

A breakdown in relationships happens when our ways of looking at the same thing conflict. We tend to dig in and create a heated argument, one against the other. We become so convinced that we are right and our partner is wrong that it becomes almost impossible to entertain an equally valid but different perspective. This can be toxic in a relationship.

Harville Hendrix likes to say, "You can be right, or you can be in relationship." Or, as Terrence Real describes in *The New Rules of Marriage*, objective reality doesn't have a place in personal relationships.

PRACTICE SHIFTING TO CURIOSITY

Together, take a look at the picture above. You may be familiar with it. It is a vivid example of how we can see very different things even when presented with the same story. Tell each other what you see. Why do some people see an old woman and others see a young woman? Discuss whether there is a correct way to see the picture. Then talk about how you would resolve a conflict if you both felt that the way you see things is right. The key is to shift from knowing to curiosity. Instead of insisting your partner is wrong and you're right, become curious about his view of the situation, ask questions, and really try to see it from his perspective. Validating your partner's perspective creates connection, which is a foundation of a healthy relationship.

28

GIVE MORE TO GET MORE

"Love recognizes no barriers. It jumps hurdles, leaps fences, penetrates walls to arrive at its destination full of hope."

Maya Angelou

ARE you someone who can subordinate your own needs and wants to attend to the needs of your partner? Can you put your partner's needs ahead of your own? That's what true, mature love actually is.

Gary Chapman, author of *The 5 Love Languages*, likes to say that love is something you do for someone else, not something you do for yourself. Our relationships will work only when we're ready to put our partner's needs ahead of our own and let go of our natural, immature, and narcissistic fixation on putting our own needs first. This type of mature love could more accurately be described as unconditional giving. It's similar to a parent's love for a child. It is the feeling of pleasure in giving that's important. You commit yourself to meeting your partner's needs and desires because you understand that she is a blueprint for your own personal growth. In other words, you understand at the deepest level that the more you give, the more you get, even when it involves a bit of stretching and doing things that are somewhat uncomfortable and inconvenient.

With this in mind, begin to experiment by noticing your reaction when your partner needs something from you. Do you feel resentful, inconvenienced, or burdened? Do you say yes but feel like saying no? Perhaps you say no and feel guilty? Do you get angry when your partner asks you to do something for her? Just notice your thoughts and how they feel in your body. In our relationship, one of the ways Craig puts Debbie's needs ahead of his is that, in the morning, he asks her, "What can I do to help make your day better?" When Craig asks this, he really means it and is always ready to stretch and meet a need.

Bottom line: the age-old truth of "the more you give, the more you get" seems to hold true in all relationships. When we want to create a giving relationship, the best strategy is to give.

PRACTICE SELFLESS GIVING

Discuss this tip and then take turns asking the following questions:

1. When do you sense that I put your needs ahead of my own?
2. When do you sense that I put my own needs ahead of yours?

After both partners ask and answer the questions, say to each other, "I would like to stretch to put your needs ahead of mine more often. In what area would that be most meaningful to you?" Listen carefully, knowing, too, that whatever your partner says is a request. Say yes only to something that you feel you can realistically do.

29

MANAGE ANGER WISELY

"Speak when you are angry and you will make the best speech you will ever regret."

Ambrose Bierce

WE frequently hear clients ask, "Don't I have the right to be angry?"

Take this scenario, for example: Wouldn't you be angry if your wife gave a friend $2,500 out of a joint savings account without asking you first? Of course, most people would. It's not the emotion of anger but how the anger is expressed that's toxic.

Craig used to try to justify his anger by saying that it was good to vent and let it out. Then, after reading *The Art of Happiness* by the Dalai Lama, he learned that venting anger is toxic and has no place in a loving relationship, and he began to look at his anger more deeply. He saw how his venting of anger had no positive benefit and only hurt his loved ones. He reflected on his personal experience and what he observed with clients and saw that the primary emotion often driving anger is hurt.

So, how do we survive these moments of anger without doing irreparable harm to our relationship? How can we nip our anger in the bud before it tears apart everything we have with our partner? The first step in dealing with our anger is to notice when it's arising. Usually, the first signals are body sensations, such as a racing heart or sweaty palms. The second step is acknowledging to ourselves that venting anger is not in the spirit of fostering understanding but comes from a harmful sense of entitlement or not feeling appreciated. Acknowledge that you are about to respond in a toxic way and instead identify positive ways to defuse the anger, such as by taking a "time-out." By doing this, you are signaling to your partner that despite your anger, the last thing you want to do is hurt your relationship.

PRACTICE MANAGING ANGER

If anger is one of your go-to responses, take some time to think about more positive ways of channeling it. Obviously, yelling, name-calling, and, worse yet, physical abuse are unhealthy. Here are some suggestions:

1. Commit to owning your anger. The solution to anger does not lie in another but only in yourself. When we get angry, a common go-to strategy is blame, which just lets us off the hook.

2. Affirm with each other your commitment to managing anger in your relationship and together develop strategies

for doing so. For example, if you are feeling flooded and need to physically leave in the middle of a conflict, instead of saying, "I am out of here!" and slamming the door, try, "I need some time to cool down, so I'm going for a run. I'll be back in thirty minutes. That would be a better time to continue this conversation."

3 If one or both you suffer from frequent and intense feelings of anger, seeking outside help is quite useful. In such cases, anger has been learned in childhood, and it is useful to explore how we learned to use anger as a response. Once we understand how anger became a habit, we can more easily transition to a healthier response when triggered.

30

NEVER SAY NEVER

"All generalizations are false, including this one."

Mark Twain

"UNIVERSAL qualifiers" is a term for words such as "never," "always," "constantly"—words that exaggerate the situation being described. They are used in blanket statements that are rarely true:

- "You *constantly* embarrass me in front of our friends."
- "*Every time* I talk you put me down."
- "You are *always* so serious."
- "It's been *forever* since we've had a date night out."
- "You *never* listen to me."
- "You are *always* shouting at the children."

None of these statements are true, yet they probably sound familiar.

Universal qualifiers are used to emphasize the merits of our own position. We use these words when we're frustrated with our partners' behavior. We start to judge and become resentful, and this creates space between us, because guess what our partners do? They get defensive and angry... and why not? Universal qualifiers are fighting words. All they do—and they do it so well—is spark a great fight!

But rarely are these statements really true *all* of the time. Let's examine one of the examples above: "You are *always* so serious."

Really? *Always*? Your partner *never* cracks a smile? Is your partner incapable of laughing at a funny movie? You have *never* seen your partner be anything but serious? Unless you are with the most serious person who ever lived, you can probably recall at least one time when he was not so serious. After all, you decided to spend time together!

One more thing to consider: although these statements are not true, they may be a true expression of your or your significant other's feelings. For example, imagine she says, "You *never* listen to me!" The truth, of course, is that you do listen, and you likely listen to her much of the time. However, when arguing, you may be missing the real message. If you listen to the underlying feeling being expressed—"I *want* to be listened to"—you will have gone beyond the hyperbole and heard something honest. If you take it one step further, perhaps you will hear, "I'm *afraid* that you may not consider me worth listening to." Now you are approaching the heart of the matter!

PRACTICE *ALWAYS* TUNING IN

Become aware of using universal qualifiers. The more you tune in to these, the more aware you will be of when you use them in a negative way in your relationship. Try this:

1. When you catch yourself using a universal qualifier, let your partner know that it is not what you meant to say. Try apologizing by saying, "I'm sorry. I didn't mean to say that you *never* support me. What I am trying to say is that *sometimes* it feels like you don't support me..." "Sometimes" is always closer to the truth.
2. If your partner uses a universal qualifier with you and it sparks a negative reaction, help her see how it may not be true. Ask her, "Is it true that I am *always* mean to you? I am *never* nice?" She may back off and say something like, "No, not *always*. I just get frustrated when you're mean—and it seems like that's a lot of the time." This is an opening to discuss what's going on. Ask your partner to tell you more and stay open to listening to the underlying need.

31

LEARN TO APOLOGIZE SKILLFULLY

"Apologizing doesn't always mean that you're wrong and the other person is right. It means that you value your relationship more than your ego."

The Gottman Institute

BREAKDOWNS in relationships are inevitable. How we deal with them defines the health and happiness of the relationship. Most of us have a hard time apologizing during times of conflict because we are more focused on why we are right and our partner is wrong. We really just want our partner to realize this and do the apologizing.

In all conflicts, we are doing something to add to the situation. Being the first to apologize is a power move. It says, "I know how to take responsibility for any breakdown, and I am willing to put my ego aside to do so." But how do we apologize? Simply saying "I'm sorry" sometimes does it, but often a little more is needed. To master the art apologizing, it's helpful to have a few techniques to draw on. Here are some possibilities:

- Say "I am sorry" with genuine emotion. A sincere "sorry" can go a long way in any conflict. The key here is the energy behind the words.
- Take responsibility by calling out exactly what you did that added to the conflict: "I am sorry. It was wrong of me to not call you when I knew my meeting was going to run late."
- Say what you will do differently next time: "In the future, I will call. I see how important it is to you."
- Reaffirm the relationship. This can be used alone or as an add-on when you take responsibility: "I am sorry. I love you, and our relationship means more to me than anything. Can we start this conversation over?" Ask for forgiveness. Sometimes our partner needs to hear the words "please forgive me."

Sometimes humor goes a long way in breaking down our resistance and restoring connection. A friend of Craig's taught him the following string of words: "I am wrong, you are right, I am sorry." For Craig, this works like a charm. There isn't much he can't get through using these words. Debbie finds them very funny, and it enables us to get past the conflict immediately or at least change the energy so we can address more clearly the core of the conflict.

Perhaps the most important tip Debbie has for apologizing is to never follow the apology with a "but." When we say "but," it negates the words that came before it, rendering our

"I am sorry" powerless. Justifications rarely land well. Say you're sorry and then just pay attention to how your partner reacts.

PRACTICE THE ART OF SAYING SORRY

Most of us could benefit from becoming well versed in the art of apology. Discuss the different ways to apologize outlined above. Separately, answer the following questions:

1. Which apology do I normally use with my partner?
2. On a scale of 1 to 5, how effective would my partner rate my technique with apologies? (1 is "terrible"; 5 is "fantastic"; 3 is "okay.")
3. What type of apology would my partner prefer?

Together, compare and discuss your answers.

32

REPAIR

"Talk to me like I'm someone you love."

Nancy Dreyfus

ALL couples argue. This is a fact. Almost all the couples that come into our offices could be diagnosed as having a "ruptured connection." No matter how careful you are, you will inevitably rupture the bond in your relationship. Even in good relationships, couples may do the following:

- Yell and scream
- Say hurtful things
- Criticize, blame, or shame
- Stonewall (withdraw from the conversation)
- Be contemptuous (put themselves on higher ground, mock each other, call each other names, roll their eyes, sneer in disgust)

The energy of an argument is "I'm right, you're wrong." If you want to shift the energy to "let's repair this rift," you must take responsibility. One way is to simply apologize. (For how to apologize, see tip 31.)

Here are some useful statements you can use to repair an argument, during or after:

- "I'm sorry. Can we start over again?"
- "When you say that, I feel..."
- "I'm sorry. I feel like my wall is up and I'm getting defensive."
- "Sorry, I didn't mean to criticize you like that."
- "I don't feel heard. Could you please repeat back what I'm saying?"
- "I know you're trying to help, but I don't need your advice right now. I just need you to be here and to listen."
- "Ouch" or any previously agreed-upon word that lets your partner know you've been hurt. This is more playful.

Debbie's favorite repair method is telling Craig she does not feel safe. She does it in a playful way, but Craig gets the point.

Sometimes arguments get so heated that no words can repair the situation. When this happens, it's best to take a time-out. Whoever calls the time-out should make sure that there is an agreement to come together again. For example, say, "I'm feeling overwhelmed. I need a break. Can we reconvene in an hour?" The time-out is part of the repair, so do it with the reassurance that you will be back and you're not rejecting or abandoning the other.

PRACTICE GOOD REPAIR

Are you effectively using repair attempts in your relationship? Google John Gottman's "Repair-Attempts Questionnaire" (or see the Sources and Resources section for a link) for a brief assessment of the effectiveness of your repair attempts. Complete the questionnaire together, taking your time with it and identifying ways you can consciously repair the next time you argue. Good repair attempts mean taking responsibility, so statements will generally include the word "I" instead of "you." Repair attempts reveal how you and your partner are feeling, and they aim to add love and connection to the conversation.

33

CREATE SOLUTIONS FOR PROBLEM AREAS

"The real act of marriage... [is] a choice you make—not just on your wedding day, but over and over again—and that choice is reflected in the way you treat your husband or wife."

Barbara De Angelis

ARGUMENTS can be about big things, or the little things can cause big arguments.

Based on our experience, here are the most common things couples seem to fight about:

- Listening/being vulnerable: Typically, arguments about listening have to do with one partner being emotionally closed off, not sharing thoughts and feelings, and not listening to and understanding what the other partner is saying. Communication is key to relationship survival.

- Finances: Several studies suggest that money may be the most common thing that couples argue about. Budgeting, spending, debt, making financial decisions, and saving habits are all concerns.
- Sex and affection: Couples will often fight about a lack of affection and a lack of expression of emotional and physical intimacy.
- Division of roles and responsibilities: Couples argue about household chores and specifically who does what. The changed roles of men and women in the workplace and the necessity for both partners to work full time influence these conflicts.
- Parenting expectations: Children can add an enormous amount of stress to a relationship. Often, parents will argue over different styles of discipline as well as parental responsibilities.
- Health and wellness: Feelings about weight gain and a lack of concern for one's health can often turn into an argument.
- Family: The jokes about in-laws tell the story. Many couples argue about the level of influence, involvement, and interference that they experience from their parents and in-laws. Family can provide great encouragement and support, yet it can sometimes undermine a relationship, if healthy boundaries are not set.
- Leisure activities: Many couples argue about the quality and quantity of their shared interests. Usually the disagreement is about not spending enough quality time together.

- Character traits: Couples often argue about a concern related to each other's character, values, or behavior, such as one person being late, not cleaning up after herself, not following through on commitments, or staying out late without calling.
- The need to be right: Oftentimes couples will argue because one person is trying to convince the other that she is just not "getting it." The truth is, there is no right or wrong, only different perspectives.

PRACTICE SOLVING FIGHTS BEFORE THEY HAPPEN

From the list above, individually select one area of disagreement that you personally would like to improve upon. Write down three things you can do to improve your relationship in this area. Make these solutions something you are willing to do and feel good about. Avoid including on this list things your partner "should" do. Share your answers and discuss. Implement the ideas you agree upon.

34

STOP THE CYCLE OF STONEWALLING

"Spiteful words can hurt your feelings, but silence breaks your heart."

C.S. Lewis

"STONEWALLING" is a term used to describe emotional withdrawal from your partner. Typically, it manifests as a refusal to answer or cooperate with your partner, speaking very little—or not at all—and quite clearly communicating that the other should stay away. It's a kind of emotional detachment that can trigger feelings of abandonment and rejection in the other. Typically, the person who withdraws—the "stonewaller"—fears escalating emotions and, in response, withholds her feelings and thoughts. Oftentimes, it just seems safer. It's a form of emotional suppression in the service of the relationship. It looks like the stonewaller doesn't care, but that is not the case. This person is often just overwhelmed and trying to calm herself. Of course, this behavior is always misinterpreted, so it doesn't work. It becomes a vicious circle, with one person demanding attention and the other just trying to escape. This is the most common pattern seen in couples who are in distress.

PRACTICE A DIFFERENT APPROACH

Here are three tips for the stonewaller:

1. Notice when you start to withdraw, shut down, or cut off contact with your partner. Then identify the underlying feelings, which may be sadness, fear, or hurt. Oftentimes the predominant motivator for stonewalling is simply feeling overwhelmed and flooded. Communicate that feeling to your partner soon after the event. For example, say, "When you said you were so mad you could tear your hair out, I felt scared and overwhelmed. I don't want to storm out, but I just don't know what else to do."
2. Rather than leaving in an angry or abrupt way, let your partner know you need a time-out and you will return. Simply say in a loving voice, "I'm a little overwhelmed; now is not a good time for me. Can we talk at [a specific time]?" Give a specific time, within the next twenty-four hours, when you'll be available to discuss your partner's concern.
3. Recognize that your partner's tendency to explode, to exaggerate his needs, or even to become aggressive is his way of reaching out to be heard and seen. He may be

afraid of losing the connection with you, and this is his clumsy way of letting you know.

Here are two tips for the pursuer:

1. Acknowledge how devalued, abandoned, or unacknowledged you feel. For example, say, "When you won't communicate with me, I feel worthless, like I'm not worth talking to." In other words, help your partner to appreciate how her stonewalling impacts you.
2. Recognize that the stonewalling is not about you; your partner simply has a different style of dealing with conflict. This is the way your partner has learned to manage her emotions, which likely has been practiced long before the two of you met. Understand that she needs to feel safe to share. Ask her if now is a good time to talk. If she says no, respect her need for space and ask her to make time for you within the next twenty-four hours.

35

TALK ABOUT MONEY WHEN THE STAKES ARE LOW

"The glow of one warm thought is to me worth more than money."

Thomas Jefferson

FINANCIAL management can be a source of great conflict for couples. These conflicts may stem from subconscious core beliefs about finances, most often learned from our parents. These early financial beliefs created our values around money and security, enjoyment and control, and they can interfere with our ability to work as a team and have financial harmony as a couple.

Since conversations about money can be very triggering, infusing lightness and curiosity into the discussion will reduce resistance and increase insight into your own and your partner's views about finances. To that end, we created the "Money Matters Game." It is designed to facilitate playful communication about important money issues.

Craig was a little nervous when we got married, because he saw Debbie as more spontaneous with respect to spending money. He pushed for meetings to discuss finances. Debbie resisted these meetings because, to her, they felt too controlling. But the request clearly communicated Craig's concern. Most of the questions in our money game came from the many discussions we had around money. Asking each other these questions opened up conversations that before had seemed more reactive than productive. Through understanding, we became more sensitive to each other on the issue and grew closer to being on the same page. We recommend trying the game, as it has been an exceptionally useful and fun activity for many of our clients.

PRACTICE THE MONEY MATTERS GAME

Play this game when you're both in a lighthearted mood, and agree that, should the mood change, you'll stop playing the game! This activity is designed for fun and insight only, and if it takes another turn, this is not the best format. Write each of the following questions on a separate piece of paper. Fold the papers up and put them in a bowl. Take turns picking questions from the bowl and answering them. Use mirroring (see "Mirroring" in the Exercises section) to be sure you're listening to your partner's answer.

1. What does money mean to you?
2. What factors influence how you spend money?

3. What factors influence how you save money?
4. What are you good at when it comes to managing money?
5. What concerns you about how you manage money? What's one thing you each could do to reduce that concern?
6. If you won $10 million, how would you spend the money?
7. What annoys you about how other people manage their money? What is the source of that annoyance?
8. What's one thing you appreciate about your partner when it comes to managing money?
9. What's one thing you're concerned about when it comes to your partner managing money? What's one thing you each could do to reduce that concern?
10. What do you say or do if you disagree with how your partner is spending money? How do these words or actions serve your relationship? How do these words or actions harm your relationship?
11. What are your greatest concerns about your future income?
12. What small, positive, mutually agreed-upon change could we make to help us better manage our money?
13. What could we agree to frivolously spend money on?

PART III

Kindling Intimacy, Sex, and Romance

36

PAY ATTENTION

Paying attention is a form of generosity.

JOHN Gottman was interested in understanding what makes some relationships work while others fail. He studied six hundred newlyweds over a period of six years. (See *The Gottman Relationship Blog* for many fascinating articles based on his research, and see the Sources and Resources section for articles pertinent to this tip.) His findings shed important light on what we can do to increase satisfaction and connection in our relationships—and what we do to destroy them.

According to Gottman, what makes the difference between relationships that do and don't thrive is how we respond to bids for attention. What's a bid for attention? Gottman defines it as any attempt from one partner for affirmation, affection, or any positive connection from the other. Bids show up in simple ways, such as a smile or wink, or more complex ways, such as requests for advice or help. Bids can also be attempts to show affection, such as a hug, a compliment, or a question about how your partner's day has been. We can respond to bids in one of three ways:

1. Turning towards: becoming curious, asking questions, and responding positively
2. Turning against: becoming argumentative and saying no
3. Turning away: ignoring or simply not seeing the bid

The subtext of most bids points to your partner's true desire. You don't have to be a mind reader; just be curious and ask questions. For example, if your partner says, "Hey, wouldn't it be fun to learn salsa dancing?" and you respond, "I don't like dancing," you've just turned away from that bid for attention, which is most likely more about spending time together than it is about dancing. To turn towards, try a response like, "I wish I liked dancing, but I don't. Can we do something else together?"

Conflict, anger, and resentment have less to do with the big issues and more to do with not getting and giving the attention needed for the relationship to survive and thrive. What if both partners took seriously these bids for attention and made it a priority to notice and respond? According to Gottman, there would be fewer divorces and way more happy, connected, and healthy relationships.

PRACTICE NOTICING

Practice noticing each other's bids for attention and consciously turning towards them. This does not necessarily mean saying yes. Turning towards means acknowledging your partner's desire for attention or support and fulfilling it somehow. You might have to say something like, "I can't talk now because I am in the middle of a project, but I would love to spend time with you later. Can we do that this evening?" Try this:

1. Together, taking turns, identify a way that you make a bid for your partner's attention. Alternate turns until neither of you can think of any other ways you make bids.
2. Over the next week, watch for possible bids for attention from each other. Have fun. Be playful. Ask your partner, "Is this a bid for attention?"
3. If your partner misses a bid, rather than expressing disappointment or resentment, just let him know that you made a bid for attention. Likewise, when he calls attention to a missed bid, take the time to ask questions and respond.
4. Most importantly, keep it light, have fun, and know that developing the habit of leaning into bids is one of the healthiest and supportive things you can do for your relationship.

37

ASK QUESTIONS TO CREATE CLOSENESS

"Anyone who knows me, should learn to know me again; for I am like the moon, you will see me with new face every day."

Rumi

CURIOSITY is about feeling like you're interested in continuing to know your partner and that they're interested in continuing to know you. Over time, people often assume they know what their partners think or feel, without really checking in. Have you ever noticed how we often answer our partners' questions for them? Being curious is about tapping into your partner's experience of the world and not assuming you know what it is.

One fundamental aspect of curiosity and intimacy is asking personal, open-ended questions rather than closed-ended questions like "How are you?" Open-ended questions are an invitation to explore thoughts and feelings. These questions don't have right or wrong answers and so create an opportunity to learn something new about your partner. Open-ended questions—such as, "What did you think about that documentary we watched?" or "What was your visit with your sister like for you?"—allow you to escape the prison of thinking you know your partner. These questions also prompt your partner to think beyond his usual parameters, which is a gift that allows the two of you to explore a new territory together.

There is evidence that emotional intimacy can be greatly accelerated by asking personal questions. According to a study by Arthur Aron and others (popularized in the article "To Fall in Love with Anyone, Do This," by Mandy Len Catron in the *New York Times*), a key pattern associated with creating an affinity between people is mutual personal self-disclosure. Asking personal questions fosters self-disclosure, thus more intimacy. Expressing curiosity about your partner is a form of kindness and generosity, communicating, "I'm genuinely interested in hearing what you have to say. I want to know what your stresses are at this moment. I want to know what can I do to make your day a little easier. I want to know what makes you feel loved and cared about. I want to know what your most embarrassing moment was as a child. I want to know your hopes and aspirations..."

Craig and Debbie have a daily ritual of asking each other at least one open-ended question, either at the end of the day or in the morning over coffee. The questions may be about current stresses, upcoming events, or anything we're interested in. But the ritual is not just about asking questions. It's about actively listening to the answers, which requires effort, attention, and focus.

Together, asking and listening demonstrates that you care—and you recognize that dynamic nature of change that exists in your partner. It says to your partner, "I know you change and grow every day and I want to share that experience with you." It says, "I want to see you."

PRACTICE CULTIVATING CURIOSITY

There are fantastic apps available that provide excellent questions and intimate conversation starters. Some of our favorites include Gottman Card Decks and 36 Questions. Download one of these to your phone, or use the list of Aron's 36 questions (see the Sources and Resources section for where to find them), and enjoy wonderful conversations with each other! Don't limit yourself to these questions, as they are simply a tool to get you started. Play with the idea and practice of asking each other open-ended questions.

38

DO THE FIFTEEN-SECOND CONNECTION

When you care about someone, make time for them.
It says, "I love you."

WE all live very busy lives filled with deadlines, appointments, and commitments that take us in many different directions throughout the day. So, it's not surprising that many of our clients sometimes find it difficult to stay connected and present. Craig and Debbie find this in their own relationship, too.

Every day and every waking moment is important. We should never take each other for granted or misuse the time that we're blessed to have with our partner and family. However, there are three specific times of the day that can hold special importance. Making the most of these times can improve even a great relationship or lay a foundation for restoring a troubled relationship. The most important times of day are before we leave for work, when we return from work, and before we go to bed.

Create a ritual of connection that takes fifteen seconds, and practice it during each of these three times. The ritual could be as simple as always stopping to greet each other with a fifteen-second kiss and embrace. Whatever you choose, the message embedded in the action is, "I love you, I see you, and I am so glad you are part of my life."

Giving fifteen seconds of loving and full attention to each other three times a day will help you to connect and increase your happiness as a couple. If you have children, there is nothing more powerful and healthy than for them to witness your love and connection. It not only makes kids feel safe, but they are learning how to connect with their partners in the future.

PRACTICE CONNECTING

Create a fifteen-second connection for the times of day listed above. How you do that is up to the two of you. Think creatively. Here are some suggestions:

- Morning connection (before you leave in the morning): Give your partner a hug and say to him, "Tell me at least one interesting thing you have planned for the day."
- Evening connection (when you return home): Formally greet each other with a hug and kiss that lasts at least fifteen seconds.

- Bedtime connection (before you go to sleep): Give an appreciation, such as, "One thing you did today that I appreciate is..." Spend a few moments cuddling and providing some physical affection.

Make this a time to enjoy each other. Change up the actions as you go along, and know that the important thing is the connection. You're creating three moments of loving connection that will boost the energy in your relationship. It's just three loving moments. You can do it!

39

ASK SEX QUESTIONS FOR BETTER SEX

"The more we trust, the farther we are able to venture."

Esther Perel

IT'S surprising how many people are not aware of their partners' sexual needs, simply because they have not asked about them. It's not that couples aren't interested, but rather that they just don't know how to approach the conversation. Yet, the most important part of cultivating a healthy sex life is being able to talk about a healthy sex life!

Have you ever tried talking about your sexual preferences? Have you ever told your partner your sexual story—the story of how you learned about sex and how you became aware of your sexuality? It's tough. It's not typical dinner table conversation, especially with kids around. And it's not something you can check off the list while running errands. Talking about sex deserves an intimate time and space—and should be a priority.

Talking comfortably with your partner about sex is strongly related to sexual satisfaction. How often couples discuss sex—as well as the quality of the conversation—is correlated with how close couples feel. The best way to open up to your partner is to ask her targeted, specific questions.

On our second date, Craig pulled out a list of questions to ask Debbie. One or two of the questions had to do with sex. Craig was surprised by how easily Debbie responded. Actually, it is usually easier to talk about sex in the beginning of a relationship. It gets more difficult as time passes and the sexual experience goes from exciting to expected. The questions change, and they can provoke feelings of insecurity, embarrassment, and vulnerability. As a result, we shy away from these conversations over time, just when we need them the most.

PRACTICE TALKING ABOUT SEX

To help you get started, we've included in the Exercises section a list of questions to spark your conversations about sex. Let these bold, brave, and explicit questions facilitate a conversation about sex—perhaps even help make the topic more comfortable to discuss. Here are a few tips for doing this exercise:

1. Set aside some time so that you can really explore these questions and listen to each other's responses.
2. Review the questions and pick out those that speak to you. There is no need to go through each one, unless you want to.

3. Take turns asking each other the questions and listen carefully, asking follow-up questions as you go along. The deeper you go, the more intimate connection you create.
4. Explore some great apps that help facilitate these conversations. Couple Game and Pillow are two we recommend (see Sources and Resources).
5. Sometimes it is helpful to create a romantic environment. Light the candles, break out the champagne, play some romantic music... and have fun connecting.

40

GAZE AT EACH OTHER

"Eye contact is more intimate than words will ever be."

Faraaz Kazi

IN a conscious relationship, one notices the importance of eye contact.

Craig was once at a Zen monastery called Tassajara, a retreat center in Northern California. During a large group sit, Craig asked a monk to explain how to be "present" in relationship, wondering if the monk would demonstrate how to do it. The monk called Craig to him and they sat face to face. With about thirty other students watching, the monk began to simply gaze into Craig's eyes, and he gazed back.

They sat silently for a few minutes, suspended in a moment when past and future seemed to fade away. They just "were." As soon as they began to speak, the spell was broken, but Craig learned a valuable lesson. Sitting quietly with your partner, not speaking, and gazing into each other's eyes, can be a powerful exercise and bring you closer to the goal of being present in your relationship. Eye gazing creates a very quiet place for you to observe your own judgments and opinions, rising and falling.

While gazing deeply into your partner's eyes, you may feel more connected to his soul, just as he will to yours. Looking in each other's eyes is a way of deepening trust and intimacy. But know that, as with many things, this isn't for everybody. Debbie has tried eye gazing, and in workshops she has even witnessed people breaking down in tears, especially when it was a person's first experience of being seen. But she finds these exercises less than transformational. We mention this not to diminish the experience but rather to highlight that we all have our own pathways. She has found that when she does this exercise to music, the connection is more powerful.

PRACTICE THAT LOOK

Before trying this exercise, watch a helpful video from SoulPancake, "How to Connect with Anyone," on YouTube (see Sources and Resources). Then turn off your smartphones, find a comfortable seat across each other, and set your timer. The length of time you choose to gaze is entirely up to you, but generally results are better when the exercise is done for five minutes or more. Here's what you do:

1. Sit quietly for a moment with your eyes closed. After quieting the mind, open your eyes and begin gazing into your partner's eyes.

2. Try to not speak during the session. Generally, your eyes may want to focus more on the left or right eye. Choose one side and let it be. The surroundings will likely begin to blur and your experience will unfold from there.
3. After your timer goes off, share with each other your experiences of eye gazing.

41

CREATE MORE SEXUAL COMPATIBILITY

"Love enjoys knowing everything about you; desire needs mystery."

Esther Perel

OFTENTIMES, in relationships, there is an incompatibility in how frequently sex is desired. One partner may want it more (the higher-sex-drive partner) and one may want it less (the lower-sex-drive partner). For most people, a mutually fulfilling sex life is incredibly important in a long-term relationship. Realizing that there is Sexual Drive Incompatibility (SDI) can be extremely frustrating.

You'll be glad to hear that SDI is quite normal in relationships and can be worked through. In fact, in long-term relationships, SDI is usually inevitable.

If you're the higher-sex-drive partner, you might find yourself doing any of the following: constantly pushing for more sex, taking personally your partner's lack of interest in having sex, and/or looking outside the relationship to meet your sexual needs.

On the other hand, if you are the lower-sex-drive partner, you need your partner to understand that you have a lower sex drive and don't want to be pressured into sex when it's not really something you desire. Oftentimes, higher-sex-drive partners forget to think about the frustration and concerns of lower-sex-drive partners, for whom it's not uncommon to feel pressure, to feel like they are letting their partners down, and to feel guilty.

When you experience sexual incompatibility in a relationship, a cycle of "the pursuer and the rejecter" may begin. The partner with the higher sex drive starts blaming and becomes demanding, critical, and resentful. The lower-sex-drive partner then tends to withdraw, feeling shamed, embarrassed, guilty, and confused.

The truth is, as time goes on, the mystery goes out of most relationships and this affects sex drive, too. The good news is that it can be revived, and when it is, it's a different type of thrill... a deeper, safer, more mature, and more satisfying mystery. Why? Because you can create it any time you want.

PRACTICE MATCHING SEX DRIVES

It's extremely important that the lower-sex-drive partner initially rule out any medical issues or medications as the cause of low sex drive. If these causes have been ruled out, have a conversation about the issue and try the following exercise together:

1. Rate your own sexual desire from 1 to 10, with 1 being "almost no desire" and 10 being "I could have it multiple times a day."

2. Lower-sex-drive partner: Identify one thing that you can do to raise your number by one. For example, schedule a time for sex when you know you'll be relaxed and rested.

3. Higher-sex-drive partner: Identify one thing you can do to create intimacy that doesn't include intercourse. For example, use toys, leave a love note, wear lingerie, use pornography, or masturbate while your partner watches and participates with soft touch and kissing.

4. Lower-sex-drive partner: Identify one thing that your partner can do more of, do less of, or continue doing to help raise your number by one. For example, take a shower with you before sex, request a certain day and time, or include light touching and massage.

42

MAKE TIME FOR EACH OTHER

How we choose to spend our time and energy tells us a lot about what we value most in life.

SCHEDULING a date night may sound irrelevant during the romantic phase of any relationship, but once children, work, parents, and other obligations enter the scene, a regular, quality date night is one of the first things to exit. We meet with many couples who would like to do more fun things together but never do. They struggle just getting the basic chores done after work and feel exhausted at the end of the day. They talk about it, even make plans, but never seem to implement them.

Sometimes one person feels like he is the one who has to plan everything, and then burnout sets in. What was once an enjoyable process of planning time together is infused with frustration and even resentment. To avoid this from happening in our relationship, we agreed to pick one night a month to plan a date from beginning to end. This allows each of us to plan a date doing what we like most. Our rule is that whatever the other person plans, we go along with it, even if it wouldn't be our choice. No criticism, no complaining. We show up to the date in an appreciative way. This way, we get to experiment with new things to do without worrying about whether the other person will like it. If one of us doesn't like it, we just choose to not do the activity again.

We often ask couples about when they spend time together, and the answer is often that they don't. Here are the three most common reasons we hear:

- No time
- Not enough money
- No child care

Our response is that date nights are always possible, but sometimes you need to get a little creative. First of all, think beyond "date night." Maybe it's "date morning" or "date afternoon." What we want you to get is some preplanned time to leave your normal stresses behind and focus on each other. This should be sacred time to honor and nurture your relationship. Committing to date night sends a message to each other that your relationship is very important.

PRACTICE DATE MORNING, AFTERNOON, OR NIGHT

Sit down with your calendars for the month. Each of you must choose one weekend day or evening to plan an activity for the two of you. If possible, spread the dates out so that they occur every other weekend. Putting them in your calendar almost guarantees that you'll have at least two dates this month, and each of you is responsible for planning only one of them. Remember, the planner has to take full responsibility for every aspect, including getting a babysitter.

Although it may seem obvious, here are a few activities to try:

- A morning hike followed by breakfast together
- A romantic movie followed by coffee and chatting about it
- A yoga class
- Bowling
- A play
- A meal at a new restaurant
- A bike ride

43

SCHEDULE SEX

Planned sex is better than no sex.

FOR most of us, keeping passion, intimacy, and hot sex alive in a long-term committed relationship is difficult. Between crazy work schedules, the kids, cleaning, laundry, and remembering to change the litter box, sex can become nonexistent—or, at best, infrequent. For busy couples with limited time, scheduling sex can ensure that you continue to have a healthy sex life.

Some say that sex should be spontaneous. They say planning it is awkward and contrived. This is a myth. We schedule everything, from doctor's appointments to drinks with friends, so why not sex? According to Tracy Moore in her article "Scheduling Sex Could Save Your Relationship—But There's a Right and Wrong Way to Do It," one study found that 36 percent of newlyweds have to schedule sex. Another study cited by Moore found that 52 percent of couples, mostly those who have kids, have to put it on the calendar. As backed by the research, some of the couples we have seen say scheduling sex has saved their relationship.

Scheduling sex may be the best way for busy couples to maintain intimacy. Rather than seeing it as an end of spontaneity, see scheduling sex as a positive component to a healthy relationship. In fact, prioritizing sex can revitalize a romance that has seen the initial enchantment wear off.

Planning sex can be exciting. For example, if you have a sex date for the evening, you can build anticipation during the day with foreplay "activities" before the main event. Put a little energy into creating some ambience and fantasize about it during the day. Maybe even send your partner a sexy text about how you are looking forward to the evening's "date."

You can also make sex a regularly scheduled ritual. When we got married, we decided to celebrate Shabbat, the Jewish Sabbath. For us, this means cooking dinner at home with the kids and sometimes friends, and it also means having sex. Having sex on Shabbat is a mitzvah, or a Jewish commandment. The underlying purpose of this commandment is to keep couples connected on a physical level, because the sages recognized how difficult this can be. When Craig came up with this idea, Debbie thought it was a little too contrived but went along because she liked the meaning behind it. It has turned out to be one of the highlights of our week. On Friday mornings, we tease each other about it, and just knowing it will happen creates anticipation and opportunities to do some planning.

The biggest mistake couples can make is to just let sex go by the wayside. After all, it is what distinguishes your relationship from a good friendship.

PRACTICE MAKING SEX DATES

Take out your calendars and plan at least one sex date per week for one month. Plan your sex date for a time when you both have the most energy and the kids won't be a distraction. Testosterone is higher for both men and women in the morning, so consider setting your alarm clock twenty minutes earlier. Other convenient times might include after a workout at the gym or between 7 and 9 p.m., before passing out.

44

TOUCH EACH OTHER

"Every gesture, every caress, every touch, every glance, every last bit of the body has its secret, which brings happiness to the person who knows how to wake it."

Hermann Hesse

HAVE you ever gone a day, a week, a month, without kissing your spouse? What about holding hands or even hugging?

We live in a busy world. Jobs, kids, bills, hobbies, and so forth eat up our waking hours. Often this leaves us with very little time left to think about, let alone lovingly touch, our significant other. And yet we know from research that touch is crucial in creating and strengthening romantic relationships. Tactile physical affection is highly correlated with overall relationship and partner satisfaction. As reported by Aaron Ben-Zeév in his *Psychology Today* article "Why a Lover's Touch Is So Powerful," conflicts are resolved more easily with increased amounts of hugging, cuddling/holding, and kissing on the lips; and, for women, receiving frequent hugs from romantic partners may significantly lower blood pressure levels. Affectionate physical behavior can also lower reactions to stressful life events. In fact, a twenty-second hug releases the bonding hormone and neurotransmitter oxytocin, which is nature's antidepressant.

In his book *The 5 Love Languages*, Gary Chapman explains that there are five ways in which a person best feels or receives love. Physical touch is one. For many couples we see, one partner's primary love language is physical touch and the other partner may come from a family where touching was not common.

The bottom line is this: initiate touch even if it is uncomfortable for you. By being mindful and taking the time to touch your partner, you're physically and emotionally demonstrating that she's a priority. The power of touch to create connection and even heal physical and emotional wounds has been well documented. If touch is not part of your relationship, you will be surprised to witness the positive effects of incorporating it.

PRACTICE AFFECTIONATE TOUCHING

Starting now, make an effort to touch your partner frequently. Here are some ideas:

- Cuddle
- Caress your partner's cheek
- Touch your partner's back as you walk past
- Fix your partner's collar or necklace

- Tickle the inside of your partner's arm
- Walk holding hands or with your arms around each other's waist
- Give a neck and shoulder massage
- Sit close enough to physically touch legs or arms
- Briefly rub your partner's back while watching TV or standing at the kitchen counter
- Play footsie with each other
- Kiss or nibble your partner's ear
- Give a soothing foot rub

With this in mind, here are some key times throughout the day when touching might be appropriate:

- When you wake up in the morning
- Before you leave for the day
- When passing each other throughout the day
- When you get home in the evening
- When you're watching TV
- Before going to sleep

45

FOCUS ON THE POSITIVE

"Keep your face to the sunshine and you cannot see a shadow."

Helen Keller

IN our practice, we find that couples have fallen into the habit of focusing on what's wrong. In Debbie's forthcoming book, she describes the importance of shifting from focusing on what is wrong to concentrating on what is right. The law of attraction states that what we give our attention to expands. Our tendency in relationships is to point out each other's faults and perhaps complain about them and then take the good for granted.

Quite simply, when we fixate on the negative, we see more negative. When we focus on the positive, we see more positive, and we also build trust, intimacy, and connection. Begin to pay attention to your ratio of negative to positive interactions with your partner. A negative interaction doesn't have to be a fight; it can simply be a negative comment.

When you catch yourself saying something negative to your partner, say at least one positive thing to balance it out. For example, if you say, "How many times do I have to ask you to drive slower?" add on something like, "I know I hassle you about speeding, but I do appreciate you always driving."

As Kyle Benson notes on *The Gottman Relationship Blog*, in his article "The Magic Relationship Ratio, According to Science," research by John Gottman and Robert Levenson shows that one primary difference between couples that stay together and those that don't is the ratio of their positive to negative interactions. Couples that stay together and report satisfaction in their relationship have more positive than negative interactions. Gottman's research suggests that this ratio is roughly five to one, positive to negative, and may actually be higher.

When couples recognize the bad habit of focusing on the negative and instead start looking for and appreciating the positive, the climate of the relationship changes. The shift from negative to positive is truly transformative, not only in our love relationships, but in our relationships with ourselves, with our kids, with other people, and with life in general.

To what extent do you tend to focus on the negative? How is that working for you? What would your life be like if you shifted that energy and instead focused on the positive?

PRACTICE THE ALPHABET GAME

We love the "Alphabet Game" because it's a fun practice of acknowledging the positive in our partner. It's equally important to practice receiving the positive, too. To play the game, find an enjoyable environment for the two of you.

Starting with the letter A, one partner chooses a positive word that describes the other—for example, "adorable." The adorable partner then expands on the word, saying something like, "I think *you're* so adorable when you wake up in the morning and say, 'I'm hungry.'" Moving on to the letter B, the adorable partner chooses a positive word for the one who started the game. Go back and forth through the entire alphabet. As always, keep it fun!

46

KEEP THE ROMANCE ALIVE

*"Always be touching her,
even when your hands cannot reach her."*

J.R. Rogue

WITH all the distractions we have in our busy lives, it seems many couples rarely find the time to be romantic, and that often leads to love's demise.

Think back to your first special joy with your partner: when you talked until the early hours of the morning, had a romantic dinner together, explored each other's bodies, took a trip together, or walked hand in hand and it didn't matter where you were or where you were going. As you recall those times, consider how you behaved towards your partner, how you looked at each other, what you were thinking, how you spoke, and how polite you were.

We often don't realize how much effort we put in at the beginning, nor do we notice our decreased effort and how that can lead to an emotional breakdown and stagnancy. Romance is a necessary part of your relationship. It says that you care about your partner and think she's worth the effort.

Having a loving conversation with your partner about what turns her on is the best way to make your relationship romantically enduring. This will take the guesswork out of it and make sure you hit a bull's-eye. What romantic gestures work for you may or may not work for your partner. It's a gift of trust when your partner takes the risk of revealing her preferences to you.

PRACTICE WOOING

Here are some tips for keeping the romance alive:

- Start with intention. Creating romance after the initial romantic phase transitions into mature love is more about intention and heart than a list of activities. When your intention is to make your partner feel special, loved, adored, and sexy, then that is exactly how she will feel. Do you have clear intentions to make each other feel like you did in the beginning of the relationship? If not, just set one. When you focus on your goals, you will naturally find the right words, activities, and ways of interacting that will make your partner feel special.
- Pay attention to what your partner likes. Does she appreciate it when you compliment her? When you cook a special meal? When, with nothing but loving intentions, you offer to help her out on a busy day? When you touch her? When you unexpectedly come home with dinner or flowers, or in a great mood? What turns your partner on?

Often we forget to pay attention, so we don't even know anymore. Start observing what really lands for your partner and do more of that. The little things you do that your partner really appreciates never get old.

- Never fail to realize the power of simply asking your partner, "What do I do that creates romance and that you really appreciate? Would you like me to do more of this?" (The answer to that may seem like an obvious yes, but ask anyhow!) Ask, "What else can I do? Is there something I can stop doing that would help create more romance?"

If you are at a complete loss for romantic things to do, do some research. We've listed a couple of wonderful books on romance in the Sources and Resources section of this book. Or Google "romantic things to do." Most importantly, be prepared to make any situation romantic!

47

SEX TOYS—TO USE OR NOT TO USE?

"And now an important message for all straight guys everywhere: some women need vibrators to get off."

Dan Savage

THE fact is, only 30 percent of women have an orgasm during intercourse. Maybe she needs more time or additional stimulation in a particular spot. The vibrator can be the best solution for creating more frequent and intense orgasms.

A lot of people either are hesitant or don't even think about using a vibrator. Just the idea of going into a sex store or shopping online can be off-putting and uncomfortable for many. One or both of you may have preconceived ideas about people who use sex toys.

Couples rarely discuss whether or not to use a vibrator. However, vibrators can improve a sex life significantly. And although it's not regularly talked about, at least one partner often wants to incorporate a vibrator or other sex toy into the sexual experience.

So, if you're interested, how do you broach the subject of using a vibrator without being concerned that you're giving your partner the wrong impression (for example, that he is not enough)?

Communication is key. It's best to approach the topic outside the bedroom, when you're both in a good mood. Talking about it ahead of time may prevent your partner from assuming he's not a good enough lover. Keep the conversation light. This is really all about making things a little more fun!

For the partner interested in using a vibrator: Sometimes people feel that a sex toy is not natural or spontaneous and that the conversation could trigger early programming about how sex should be. It also could be that your partner secretly desires something new but is hesitant to bring it up. Or maybe he's more open than you think. Either way, when you initiate this conversation, make it light.

For the partner who may not be interested in using a vibrator: If your partner wants to introduce a sex toy, be open and try to really listen. Someone who desires to use sex toys should be able to communicate that without feeling judged or shamed. If there's a good sex shop where you live, the next time the two of you walk by it, *go in*! You don't have to buy anything; just enjoy looking at the merchandise. Or go online together and research various sex toys. Talk about which ones you'd like to try, and perhaps go out on a limb and order one!

Have fun exploring toys to spice up your sex life, but always remember that they are not a replacement for human touch, cuddling, affection, and connection. They are simply a way to enhance your experience.

PRACTICE TALKING ABOUT TOYS

Together, discuss bringing a vibrator or any other sex toys into the bedroom. Before you do, create an atmosphere conducive to having a satisfying, playful, and romantic sex conversation. Consider a bottle of wine, some candles, and romantic music. Then ask each other the following questions (or make up your own):

1. Would you be comfortable bringing a vibrator or another sex toy into the bedroom and experimenting with it together?
2. Have you ever used a sex toy with yourself?
3. Have you ever used a sex toy with another person?
4. Are there any specific sex toys you'd like to consider?
5. Are there any specific sex toys you would never consider? Why?

48

MAKE VACATIONS ROMANTIC

"Though we travel the world over to find the beautiful, we must carry it with us or we find it not."

Ralph Waldo Emerson

MOST of us anticipate our next vacation with excitement. While creating an itinerary, navigating an unfamiliar place, and sticking to a budget, couples sometimes find that romance takes a back seat to practicality.

We find that most couples—especially those with young children—never consciously think about making vacations romantic. Consequently, you may be sitting in a secret garden café overlooking the sea and a spectacular sunset with your eyes glued to your phones as you search the internet for tomorrow's activities. Romance completely disappears.

Despite the toils of traveling, making romance on the road isn't as difficult as it may seem. Draw up a list of the most romantic places to visit, and consider booking a trip to one. There's no need to spend thousands of dollars on a weekend getaway or to persuade foreign hotel staff to leave rose petals on your bed in the shape of your partner's face. Spice up your love life with unique and inexpensive ways to add some intrigue to your vacation. Here are some suggestions:

- Bring clothes that you know your partner enjoys seeing you in.
- Plan a surprise romantic dinner at a special place. Surprises are very effective in creating romance.
- Look for the little things to compliment your partner on.
- Flirt! Let your eyes say, "You are so sexy and I'm thrilled be sharing this moment with you."
- Hold hands a lot! There's nothing like physical connection to make you feel the emotional connection.
- Pamper yourselves. For example, indulge in a soothing body massage after you're done with sightseeing for the day. Treat yourselves to a rejuvenating experience.

PRACTICE SPICING UP TRAVEL

Above are some pointers for activities for your time away together. But you can also enjoy preparing in advance. Here are some steps for spicing up travel:

1. Plan romantic and fun activities. As an exercise, individually write down five things that you would like to do on a trip to make it more romantic. Then, together, compare your lists and agree on what you'll do on your next trip.

2. Anticipate and work around possible breakdowns. We often observe that while vacations are meant to add romance to our lives, they have the potential of doing the opposite. Sit down with your partner and identify a couple of things that could potentially go wrong and plan around them. What we hear from our couples, and know through our own experience, is that a lack of presence represents one of the biggest breakdowns on vacations. Here are some of the most common concerns we hear:

    - "I just want him to be present and not on his phone doing business every day."
    - "I just want to relax on the beach and recharge, and he, once again, overbooked us."
    - "I want to feel like I have his undivided attention, and he is always trying to connect with strangers."
    - "I want to sleep in and order breakfast in bed, and he wants to go for a long run and so leaves me on my own every morning."

What breakdowns are you likely to face? Together, what can you do to create romance instead of disappointment? A little planning goes a long way. The key is always compromise. When each partner stretches a little for the sake of the other, romance will naturally result.

49

CREATE RELATIONSHIP SATISFACTION WHILE RAISING CHILDREN

"The most important thing a father can do for his children is to love their mother."

Theodore Hesburgh

It seems obvious that adding a baby to a household is going to change its dynamics. Indeed, the arrival of children shifts how couples interact. Parents often become more distant and businesslike with each other as they attend to the details of raising a child. Mundane basics like feeding, bathing, and clothing children take energy, time, and resolve. To keep the family running smoothly, parents discuss car-pool pickups and grocery runs instead of connecting with each other. New parents tend to stop saying and doing the little things that please their partners. Questions about each other's day are replaced with questions about whether this diaper looks full. Flirty texts are replaced with messages that read like a grocery receipt.

These changes can be profound. Fundamental identities may shift—at an intimate level—from lovers to parents. Simply put, the arrival of children predicts less relationship satisfaction and sex. Yet, despite the dismal picture of motherhood we often hear about, most mothers (and fathers) rate parenting as their greatest joy. Most women believe the rewards of watching their children grow up are worth the cost to their romantic relationships, as well as the pain and suffering of childbirth. But how do we manage being both parents and partners?

PRACTICE BEING LOVERS WHO HAVE CHILDREN

Spending time together as a couple is vital to the health of your relationship. Here are eight suggestions for maintaining a high level of relationship satisfaction while raising children:

1. Have a date night every week. It doesn't have to be a full-on fancy night out. Just carve out some time for the two of you to catch up. (And, by the way, turn off your phones.)

2. Spend fifteen minutes a day checking in with each other. Catching up with your partner helps to keep you emotionally and intimately connected.

3. Have sex. If necessary, schedule sex into your calendar (see tip 43). At a minimum, make time for cuddling!

4. Share housework. Parents often fight about the division of labor and who does what. Be proactive. Come up with a plan that you both feel good about.
5. Take a parenting class together. Many couples are just not on the same page when it comes to parenting. There are more decisions and usually more differences of opinion to negotiate than ever before.
6. Take a relationship skills class together. A strong relationship is much more likely to weather the stress of having children.
7. Take a Prepare/Enrich parenting assessment and review it with a trained facilitator. This parenting assessment is designed to guide couples through the emotions of parenting by empowering them with insight into their parenting style and family dynamics. (See craiglambert therapy.com/prepare-and-enrich-assessment/.)
8. Notice what your partner does right. With the stress of parenting, it's easy to focus on what your partner does wrong. Instead, appreciate what they do right as a parent.

50

HAVE MORE FUN TOGETHER

"We don't stop playing because we grow old;
we grow old because we stop playing!"

George Bernard Shaw

ARE you fun-impaired? Sometimes Craig thinks he is. He often prefers to sit at home, browsing the internet and working. He likes the focused attention and quiet. Debbie wouldn't say Craig is fun-impaired, because he's very lively when he gets out from behind his desk. When he and Debbie were dating, Craig jumped out a window pretending to be a fisherman. It was hysterical and it revealed a side of him that knows how to play.

Fun is one of the most important, underrated ingredients in any relationship. Our relationships should be serious no more than 25 percent of the time, while the rest should be lighthearted and pleasurable. Life can be difficult enough as it is. When we choose to engage with someone, let it be a person who lightens our load rather than adds to it. Healthy relationships always have more comedy than drama!

Think about when you and your partner started dating. You probably spent a significant amount of time doing enjoyable activities intending to keep them alive forever. When relationships begin, fun is more natural and effortless, but over time it becomes easier to take things for granted. Also, circumstances such as kids, household chores, long work hours, and everyday challenges get in the way of a couple's leisure time.

So, how do we add more fun to our relationships? It's most likely to happen when we do two things: plan for it (see the practice below) and set a daily intention to have fun. Simply wake up in the morning and say to yourself, "I am going to keep it light today and find the humor in whatever I see. Life is short and I choose to skip through it rather than walk heavy. When I interact with my partner, I will keep it light, loving, and connected. I will do more smiling and laughing and point out the funny rather than the scary. I will play with my partner in simple ways that we both appreciate."

When Debbie and her father used to talk on the phone, he would tell jokes and stories until she laughed. Then he would say, "Aw, I made you laugh. Now I can go." Having the intention to make the other smile, laugh, have fun... this is the gift every relationship needs.

PRACTICE PRIORITY NUMBER ONE—FUN

Make having fun a priority, and keep it light. After all, we are talking about having fun! Here's a simple exercise to bring more fun and lightness into your lives:

1. Together, discuss the question, "What obstacles to having fun are we facing and what are we willing to do about it?"
2. Individually, write down at least ten activities you would like to do with your partner. (See the "Fun Activities List" in the Exercises section for inspiration.) Consider fun things you've done before and want to do again, as well as completely new activities. Brainstorm without limits. Don't worry about costs or whether your partner is willing to do it or not.
3. Share your lists with each other. Each of you pick one thing from the other's list and schedule some fun time. Agree on dates and times, and put them in your calendar.

51

KEEP YOUR SEX LIFE ALIVE

"Sex is about where you can take me,
not what you can do to me."

Esther Perel

MANY of the couples we work with have sex infrequently or not at all. So, what do sexually satisfied couples do to keep a strong sex life alive? Here is a list of eight behaviors of couples who enjoy a healthy sex life:

1. They have sex. It sounds obvious, but sex begets more sex. Without forcing it, coax yourself to engage sexually even if you don't feel like it. Orgasms release a neurotransmitter called dopamine, and snuggling after sex releases a hormone called oxytocin. These chemicals create a kind of relationship glue by creating feelings of love, euphoria, and desire.

2. They have sex at least once a week. It turns out the benefits of sex level off after once a week. In one study it was found that couples who have sex four times a week have the same level of marital satisfaction as those who have sex once a week. Many couples feel pressured to have as much sex as possible, which can backfire. They feel so overwhelmed that they avoid it entirely. Ultimately, it's the quality, not the quantity, of sex that truly counts.

3. They are motivated to meet their partner's sexual desires, even when they don't feel like it. Couples are not always in sync: very often, one wants to and the other doesn't; one prefers a particular position that the other doesn't like; one prefers more romance and foreplay, and the other can go without it. If your partner wants sex, do it. If your partner has particular preferences that are not yours, stretch and indulge her sometimes. You will most likely feel better for doing so.

4. They are attentive to each other's emotional needs outside the bedroom. Many studies have shown that those who feel their partners are responsive to their emotional needs report a higher sex drive.

5. They say "I love you" during sexual encounters. Saying "I love you" helps you to bond psychologically.

6. They divvy up housework and errands fairly equally. Couples who share these responsibilities have far more frequent and satisfying sex. By sharing the daily load, you create an environment of giving, which creates intimacy.

7. They engage in adrenaline-raising, novel activities. In fact, any fun activity you do with your partner can help bring back the sexual spark.

8 They embrace sexual variety. Try new positions, a bath together, giving each other massages, or sharing and acting out a fantasy. Keep it interesting and you'll find more satisfaction.

PRACTICE GETTING SEXY

Sit down together and talk about the eight behaviors that define a healthy sex life. Is there something from the list that's missing from your relationship? Decide what behaviors make sense for you to add or do more of. Start with one thing and, a week or so later, try something else that's new. Enjoy yourselves!

52

LOOK, AND SEE

"Intimacy is not purely physical: it is the act of connecting with someone so deeply you feel like you can see into their soul."

Reshall Varsos

EMOTIONAL intimacy, or "into-me-you-see," is that sense of closeness we feel with our partners when we are vulnerable and allow ourselves to be seen. Emotional intimacy requires a safe space for sharing our personal thoughts and feelings, our compassion and caring. Creating that space can be difficult in our overcommitted, work-focused, child-focused culture. We have found that emotional intimacy depends on several relationship skills or habits. To foster emotional intimacy, we need to do the following:

- Be vulnerable. We need to feel safe enough to openly share our deepest thoughts and feelings. Being vulnerable means being courageous enough to be seen.

- Feel that our partners lovingly accept our thoughts and feelings.
- Listen to our partners' thoughts and feelings, without judgment or giving unwanted advice. Hold them in warm regard despite any disagreements or negative judgments we have.
- Practice emotional containment (see tip 15)—that is, hold our own highly charged feelings, while at the same time remaining connected. Being present for our partners is an act of trust. They trust us to hear what they have to say, without insulting, criticizing, shaming, or blaming them. Meanwhile, they recognize that we may be triggered by what they say, and they trust us to not act out but, instead, to show up with curiosity and love. This requires that, together, we talk about problems as soon as they arise and express our concerns in a balanced, mature way.
- Show our partners how much we care, including by expressing affirmations, appreciations, and loving behaviors.

PRACTICE "INTO-ME-YOU-SEE"

Sit close, perhaps even knee-to-knee, facing each other, holding hands. This simple touching creates an atmosphere of mutual acceptance. Try any or all of the following:

1. Take turns expressing appreciation and saying thank you for something your partner has done.
2. Take turns sharing things the other doesn't already know about you and letting your partner in on your mood, your experiences, and your life.

3. Take turns asking each other about something you don't understand, allowing the speaker time to explain. For example, "Why were you so down last night?" Or voice a question about yourself: "I don't know why I got so angry while we were figuring out expenses." You might not have answers, but be willing to give your partner some insight into you. And you may have insights about each other.

4. Without placing blame or being judgmental, cite a specific behavior that bothers you, and state the behavior you're asking for instead. For example, "If you're going to be late for dinner, please call me. That way the kids and I can make our own plans and we won't be waiting for you."

5. Share your hopes and dreams. This is integral to a relationship. Hopes can range from the mundane ("I hope you don't have to work this weekend") to the grandiose ("I'd really love to spend a month in Europe with you"). The more the two of you bring hopes and dreams into immediate awareness, the more likely you'll find a way to realize them.

A NOTE ON THE DEDICATIONS

CRAIG

I have dedicated this book first to my mom, Faith Lambert. My mother was a fantastic role model for how to be in a relationship, not so much with my dad (they divorced when I was six) but with her second husband, her children, and her friends. She was a great communicator and put a premium on the importance of sharing feelings. She was a superb listener. In fact, she taught me to be a great listener and to question, empathize, and validate. She always encouraged me to share my feelings. When I arrived home from school, she always asked me how I was feeling. I would answer, like most people, "Fine." Then she would stop me and say, "How are you really feeling?" These words stopped me in my tracks, as I felt like she really wanted to know and was not simply asking to be polite. When I answered, she became very curious and asked open-ended questions that helped me explore my feelings even more. She always validated my perspective and understood how I was feeling. Her good advice came later, after she had helped me explore my own thoughts and feeling about the issue. Her compassion knew no bounds. Her constant encouragement for me to feel my feelings shaped me quite differently compared with most of my male friends, who were learning to cover theirs up. I always thought my mom would have made an excellent therapist, and this book and these tips, in one way or another, came from her. She would have loved this book. She would have been very proud that her son and his wife wrote it.

I am most happy that, before my mother died, she had a chance to meet Debbie. My mom adored Debbie and the two of them developed a special bond in a very short period of time. I would also like to express my deep gratitude to Debbie. Her love, her wisdom, her sense of humor, and her common sense brought a perspective to this book that could only be described as wise and inspired.

DEBBIE

I have dedicated this book to my dad. Unlike Craig's mom, my father was pretty much cut off from his feelings. He was raised in a ghetto in Poland and, at the age of nineteen, came to the United States with two other siblings to work and make enough money to bring the rest of the family to America. Unfortunately, that never happened, as the war broke out and he lost both parents and five other siblings. My dad learned that feelings were nonessential and that the goal in life is to work hard and to provide. That he did, and he did so much more. What my dad brought to the table was his sense of humor and lightness. This was particularly inspiring given the hardship that colored his life. He taught me that a laugh and a smile are maybe the best gifts you can give someone. He taught me, above all else, be generous, and he modeled the way every day, with my mom, with my sister and me, with his customers, with his friends, and with anybody who had the gift of knowing him. Even in his final days, he made us laugh because his philosophy was to live the best life you can, for it is a short ride, so enjoy it. I thank my dad for giving me the gift of humor and lightness, and with each smile and each laugh, I remember him.

I also express the deepest thanks to Craig, because he picked up where my dad left off. Craig taught me that, no matter what I am feeling, it is important to share; and he is gifted in creating a safe and loving space for anyone willing to open up. I learned from Craig the importance of asking questions and I am inspired as I watch him transform what could be very light conversations into deeply loving and connected ones. I witness this with his kids, his friends, his family, and certainly in our relationship. My life is so much richer since meeting him and I'm grateful for every day we spend together. I am grateful not only for the love that we share but for the opportunity of co-creating with the man I love.

ACKNOWLEDGMENTS

YOU KNOW HOW, during the Academy Awards, first-time award-winners get up and have so many people to acknowledge that they just don't hear the music that says, "Your time is up"? That is a little bit how we feel when trying to figure out who to acknowledge, because the reality is that so many people have influenced and touched us in ways that are deeply meaningful.

We would like to start by acknowledging our teachers who came before us with content so rich it moved us in ways we cannot express. In the area of couples work, there is Harville Hendrix and Helen LaKelly Hunt, Terry Real, Esther Perel, John Gottman, and Sue Johnson, to name a few.

Spiritual leaders who have influenced our thinking and touched our hearts include our teacher Light, Ram Dass, Abraham Hicks, Byron Katie, Eckhart Tolle, Joko Beck, B.K.S. Iyengar, and dozens more.

Craig has a long-standing men's group, including Mathew Fink, Brian Hext, and Mark Loekemper. It has provided ongoing support for many years. They show him that men can be vulnerable and intimate with each other and, when they are, it's beautiful.

In life, you get a few friends who feel more like soul mates. We are blessed with many, including the entire Church family, Patti and Steve Aretz, Hal and Carly Michaels, Aman and Sunny Keays—all who have shown us what beautiful relationships look like.

We both want to acknowledge with gratitude our previous spouses, who helped us perhaps more than anyone to understand the trials and tribulations of being in relationships; in that regard, we acknowledge Louise, Colin, and Jan.

Thank you to Craig's father, for his constant caring and the love that we feel in his voice and in his hugs. Our siblings, Scott, Andrea, Tiffany, and Trudy, who remind us of our history together and how easy it is to feel the deep connection, even when time and distance creates space in the relationship.

Last, but certainly not least, we would like to acknowledge our children: JB, who always reminds us how to hold the sacred space of the downtrodden and how to truly connect in a loving way every day; Gage, whom we can always count on to help us look outside the box and challenge our decisions and assumptions; Shayna, who makes us laugh with her quick wit and inspires us with her courageousness to explore her own edge, always trying to understand herself and the world; Sophie, who demonstrates great courage, intellect, and poise in the face of life challenges; and Emma, whose free and loving spirit is a gift to everything she touches, including the plants, the herbs, the animals.

EXERCISES

THE FOLLOWING EXERCISES and lists support several "practices" we've suggested in the tips and, in general, will help you build trust and closeness in your relationship.

IDENTIFY YOUR FEELINGS

Review this list of feelings when you need help identifying and expressing yourself to your partner and when you need help identifying with your partner's emotions.

AFFECTIONATE (compassionate, friendly, loving, open-hearted, sympathetic, tender, warm)

AFRAID (apprehensive, filled with dread or foreboding, frightened, mistrustful, panicked, petrified, scared, suspicious, terrified, wary, worried)

AGITATED (alarmed, disturbed, rattled, shocked, startled, troubled, in turmoil, uncomfortable, unnerved, unsettled, upset)

ANGRY (enraged, furious, incensed, indignant, irate, livid, outraged, resentful)

ANNOYED (aggravated, dismayed, disgruntled, displeased, exasperated, frustrated, impatient, irritated, irked)

CONFIDENT (empowered, open, proud, safe, secure)

CONFUSED (ambivalent, baffled, bewildered, dazed, mystified, perplexed, puzzled, torn)

CONTEMPT (filled with animosity, appalled, disgusted, horrified, hostile, repulsed)

DISCONNECTED (alienated, apathetic, bored, cold, detached, distant, distracted, indifferent, numb, uninterested, withdrawn)

EMBARRASSED (ashamed, chagrined, flustered, guilty, mortified, self-conscious)

ENGAGED (absorbed, alert, curious, engrossed, enchanted, entranced, fascinated, interested, intrigued, involved, stimulated)

EXCITED (amazed, animated, ardent, aroused, astonished, eager, energetic, enthusiastic, giddy, invigorated, lively, passionate, surprised, vibrant)

EXHILARATED (ecstatic, elated, enthralled, exuberant, radiant, rapturous, thrilled)

FATIGUED (beat, burnt out, depleted, exhausted, lethargic, listless, sleepy, tired, weary, worn out)

GRATEFUL (appreciative, moved, thankful, touched)

HOPEFUL (encouraged, optimistic)

INSPIRED (awed, wonderstruck)

JOYFUL (amused, delighted, glad, happy, jubilant, pleased, tickled)

PAIN (in agony, anguished, bereaved, devastated, filled with grief, heartbroken, hurt, lonely, miserable, remorseful)

PEACEFUL (calm, clearheaded, comfortable, centered, content, fulfilled, mellow, quiet, relaxed, relieved, satisfied, serene, still, tranquil, trusting)

REFRESHED (enlivened, rejuvenated, renewed, rested, restored, revived)

SAD (depressed, dejected, despairing, despondent, disappointed, discouraged, disheartened, forlorn, heavy-hearted, hopeless, melancholy, unhappy)

TENSE (anxious, cranky, distressed, distraught, edgy, fidgety, frazzled, irritable, jittery, nervous, overwhelmed, restless, stressed out)

VULNERABLE (fragile, guarded, helpless, insecure, leery, reserved, sensitive, shaky)

YEARNING (envious, jealous, longing, nostalgic, wistful)

CO-CREATING A RELATIONSHIP VISION

Write down the following categories: time together, love and intimacy, spirituality, work, finances, communication, friends and family, and health. Then try this:

1. Under each category, individually, write down short sentences that describe your personal vision of the relationship you want. Write each sentence in the present tense, as if it were already happening. For example: "We have fun together"; "We are loving parents"; "We hug a lot"; "We respect each other"; "We rely on and trust each other."

Write at least two vision statements under each category. Let your imagination go wild. Once you have finished creating your vision statements, read them out loud to each other, taking turns with alternating lines and mirroring back what your partner says.

2. When all the items have been read and mirrored accurately, compare the two lists. Whenever you identify similar items, place a check mark next to the items that you both listed. It doesn't matter if you use different words as long as the general idea is the same. If your partner has written anything that you agree with or do not object to but that you did not think of yourself, add it to your list as you go. Each of you then places a check mark next to it. If your partner has written items with which you do not agree, do not discuss them at this time. Draw a thick line below these items. Your differences are options for future dialogue.

3. Combine the two separate visions, including all the agreed-upon items. When you have finished co-creating your mutual vision, read it out loud to each other, taking turns with alternating lines. This is a live document, so together you can add or subtract anything, as long as you agree on it. It's not carved in stone.

MIRRORING

In many of the practices in this book, you will benefit from your ability to mirror each other. Mirroring is the process of listening carefully to your partner and accurately reflecting back the content of her message. This means repeating back what your partner said, without interpreting, distorting, emphasizing, adding to, or selecting out what is important. It also means reflecting back the tone and intensity of the sender without mimicking. Initially, it may feel mechanical, slow, and awkward, but deep listening is like learning to ride a bicycle… eventually, it becomes much more fluid.

These conversations require undivided attention. It's important to make sure that both parties are in the right emotional and physical space to mirror… so always check in with your partner: "Is now a good time?" Asking this simple question respects your partner's emotional space and prevents you from feeling rejected or deflated by a partner who may not be available at the moment. To mirror, the sender does the following:

- Speaks her message as simply and concisely as possible
- Begins the initial sentence with an "I" statement ("I need," "I feel") and avoids blame, shame, or criticism

The receiver must do the following:

- Listen to the sender and then accurately mirror the message back ("Let me see if I've got you? You said…")
- After mirroring, check for accuracy by asking, "Did I get that right?"
- Keep asking, "Is there more?" until the sender says, "No. That's it."
- Summarize the key points that the sender just shared ("In summary, what I hear you saying is…")

It is important for the receiver to control the content flow to more easily and accurately mirror back. To stop your partner from talking, simply raise your hand and say "pause" or "stop." Mirror what you heard, check for accuracy, and then ask your partner to continue. Call this the "pause button."

During a mirroring exercise is not the time to respond. Receivers need to suspend their personal perspectives, judgments, or opinions and be open to hearing their partners' point of view. Receivers must have the capacity to contain reactions and responses and allow their partners to be the center, temporarily, letting it just be about them.

"Is there more?" is one of the most powerful questions a partner can ask. It says something that we seldom hear from anyone: "I have time for you. I want to listen, and I want to know your thoughts."

VALIDATION

Validation is a communication to your partner that the information you are receiving and mirroring "makes sense." It indicates that you can see your partner's point of view and can accept its validity—it is true for your partner. In other words, when mirroring, you don't say, "That's not true."

Validation is a temporary suspension or transcendence of your own perspective that allows your partner's experience to have its own reality. Validation conveys to your partner that you know that her subjective experience is as valid as your own.

To validate your partner's message does not mean that you agree with her perception or that it reflects your subjective experience. It merely recognizes that in any communication between two people, there are always two views, that no "objective view" is possible, and that any report of an experience is an interpretation, which is the "truth" for each person. Validation enables two different perspectives to coexist safely. The process of mirroring and validation affirms the other person and increases trust, safety, closeness, connection, and your capacity for empathy. Here are some examples of validation:

- "What you're saying makes sense to me."
- "I follow what you're saying and you make sense."
- "You make sense to me."
- "What makes sense is..." (This a powerful validating phrase as it specifies what exactly makes sense.)

EMPATHY

Empathy is imagining, reflecting, and on some level experiencing the emotions that your partner is feeling. Empathy is listening with your heart. Where validation is truly hearing the ideas, empathy is feeling the emotions a person is communicating.

It creates kindness, compassion, safety, and vulnerability, thus allowing you to experience a genuine connection. You imagine the feelings of your partner by momentarily stepping into his experience to feel his pain, anger, fear, appreciation, or joy.

Very often people describe thoughts but call them feelings. For example, the sentence "You feel that you don't want to go with me" describes a thought, not a feeling, whereas "You're sad because you're too tired to go with me" describes a feeling. By empathizing and participating in the feelings that your partner is discussing, you deepen the level of connection and transcend your separateness. Here is a sequence for expressing empathy:

- "It sounds like you're feeling..." (Complete the sentence with an emotion [see "Identify Your Feelings" above]. This will draw on your capacity for empathy.)

- "Is that what you're feeling?"
- If your partner corrects you, mirror back the correct feeling. (For example, your partner says, "No, I am actually feeling relieved." And you say, "So you are feeling relieved.")...

QUESTIONS TO SPARK A CONVERSATION ABOUT SEX

This is by no means a comprehensive list. Consider each question a jumping-off point, created with the hope that you will elaborate on each question and ask follow-up questions. Have fun!

1. On a scale of 1 to 10, how comfortable are you discussing sexual issues, including wants, likes, and dislikes, with me (with 1 being "not at all" and 10 being "100 percent comfortable")?
2. What does intimacy mean to you?
3. Do you feel comfortable sharing your needs for affection with me?
4. Describe a time when I gave you affection that made you feel loved.
5. What is one new way that I can demonstrate affection for you?
6. Do you have a sexual preference or expectation that would be helpful for us to discuss?

7. Are you comfortable with our current level of sexual activity? Would you prefer slightly more, slightly less, a lot more, or a lot less?
8. Is there an event in your sexual history that stands out for you and that I may not know about, yet it may influence your sexuality?
9. What's forbidden for you sexually?
10. What turns you on sexually?
11. What turns you off sexually?
12. What is one thing around sexuality that you struggle with?
13. What is your favorite position?
14. Something I would like to change in relationship to my sexuality is... (e.g., I'd like to be less inhibited, more romantic, more spontaneous, more sensitive, more playful, and so on).
15. Do you distinguish between making love and having sex?
16. How do you feel about talking when we make love? How about making noises?
17. What is your preferred time of day to make love?
18. What do you enjoy most when we make love?
19. Do you like sex toys? Would you like to use them together?
20. As we grow older, do you believe the best is yet to come or has it already passed?

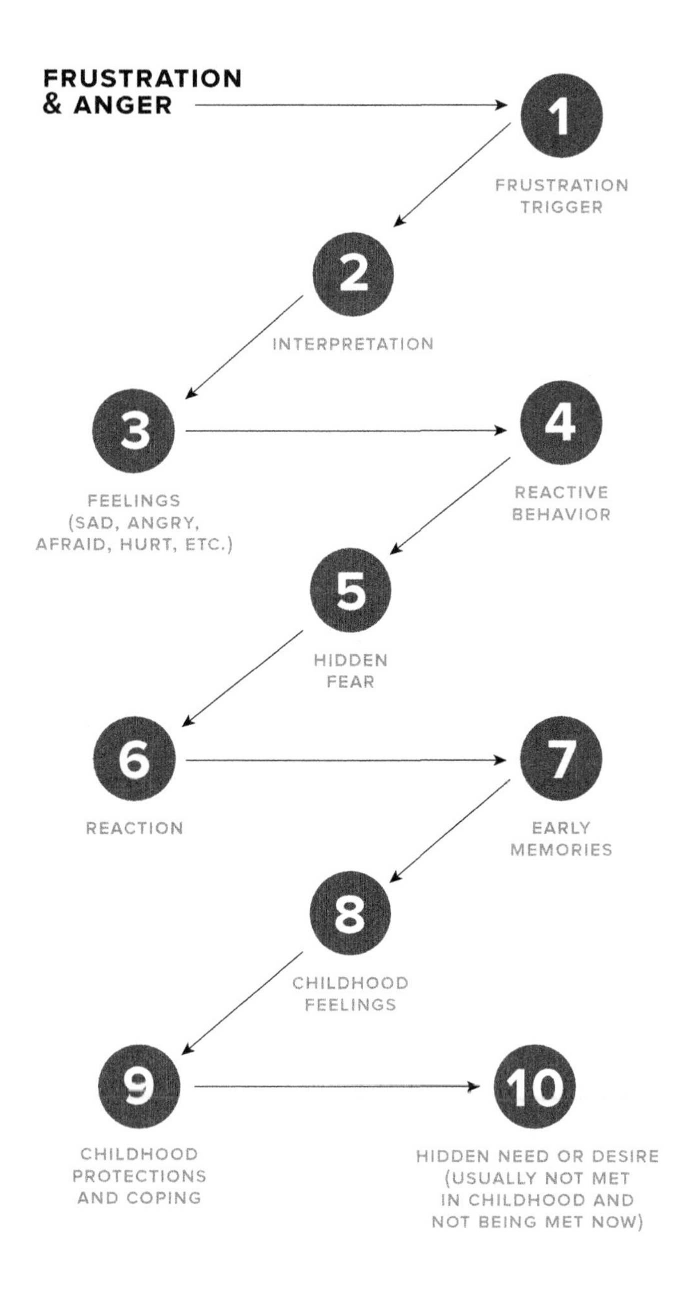

FRUSTRATION & ANGER
1
FRUSTRATION TRIGGER
2
INTERPRETATION
3
FEELINGS (SAD, ANGRY, AFRAID, HURT, ETC.)
4
REACTIVE BEHAVIOR
5
HIDDEN FEAR
6
REACTION
7
EARLY MEMORIES
8
CHILDHOOD FEELINGS
9
CHILDHOOD PROTECTIONS AND COPING
10
HIDDEN NEED OR DESIRE (USUALLY NOT MET IN CHILDHOOD AND NOT BEING MET NOW)

DECONSTRUCTING FRUSTRATION AND ANGER

1. FRUSTRATION TRIGGER
   "What upsets or frustrates me is..."

2. INTERPRETATION
   "When this happens, the story I tell myself is..."

3. FEELINGS (SAD, ANGRY, AFRAID, HURT, ETC.)
   "My deepest pain is..."

4. REACTIVE BEHAVIOR
   - "My first reaction is..."
   - "And then I..."

5. HIDDEN FEAR
   "My deepest fear is..."

6. REACTION
   "Then I react by..."

7. EARLY MEMORIES
   "This reminds me of..." (painful childhood memory, or a prior relationship pain)

8. CHILDHOOD FEELINGS
   "My deepest pain then was..."

9. CHILDHOOD PROTECTIONS AND COPING
   "I learned to cope and protect myself by..."

10. HIDDEN NEED OR DESIRE (USUALLY NOT MET IN CHILDHOOD AND NOT BEING MET NOW)
    "To help me heal from all that [childhood pain or from my ex], what I need from you is..." (Be specific in the request.)

FUN ACTIVITIES LIST

- ◯ Try new ethnic cuisine
- ◯ Sightsee around your own city
- ◯ Play Frisbee
- ◯ Fly a kite
- ◯ Go to an outdoor theater performance
- ◯ Go skating
- ◯ Take a mystery trip/get in your car and drive
- ◯ Go to a go-kart track
- ◯ Go to a driving range
- ◯ Go to an amusement park
- ◯ Attend a murder mystery dinner show
- ◯ Visit an aquarium
- ◯ Go to a sports game
- ◯ Do a restaurant tour
- ◯ Browse an antique store or a flea market
- ◯ Explore the nearest state park
- ◯ Rent a kayak, rowboat, or sailboat
- ◯ Rent bikes
- ◯ Attend a music festival
- ◯ Eat at a new restaurant

- ◯ Go stargazing
- ◯ Take a dinner cruise
- ◯ Have an indoor picnic
- ◯ Visit a museum
- ◯ Learn a new activity together
- ◯ Go to an art gallery
- ◯ Make breakfast in bed
- ◯ Go bowling
- ◯ Go on a hike
- ◯ Play bingo
- ◯ Go horseback riding
- ◯ Create a couples' scrapbook
- ◯ Host a couples' game night
- ◯ Create a music playlist of your relationship
- ◯ Go on a hot air balloon ride
- ◯ Attend a concert you will both enjoy
- ◯ Read the same book at the same time and discuss
- ◯ Go to the beach
- ◯ Play twenty questions
- ◯ Complete a jigsaw puzzle together
- ◯ Take a staycation

- ◯ Dine out at a fancy restaurant
- ◯ Take a horse carriage ride
- ◯ Run a race together
- ◯ Put on music and dance at home, perhaps make it a slow dance
- ◯ Go camping
- ◯ Go skinny dipping
- ◯ Cook a meal together
- ◯ Cuddle by the fire
- ◯ Go wine tasting
- ◯ Sing a karaoke duet together
- ◯ Take a trip somewhere new
- ◯ "Sext" each other
- ◯ Volunteer together
- ◯ Dress up in a couples' costume for Halloween
- ◯ Start a new tradition together
- ◯ Play miniature golf
- ◯ Sleep under the stars
- ◯ Watch both the sunrise and sunset the same day
- ◯ Take a bubble bath while enjoying champagne and strawberries
- ◯ Get a couples' massage

- ◯ Have a tech-free date day together
- ◯ Go on a double date
- ◯ Play a sexy game of Twister
- ◯ Visit each other's hometowns
- ◯ Take a workout class together
- ◯ Do a movie marathon
- ◯ Get naughty in every room of your house
- ◯ Stay up all night
- ◯ Binge-watch a new TV series
- ◯ Have a casino night
- ◯ Go on a brewery tour
- ◯ Play hide-and-seek
- ◯ Play Ping-Pong
- ◯ Practice *Kama Sutra* sex positions
- ◯ Find the best happy hour in town and make the appetizers your meal
- ◯ Play strip poker
- ◯ Go to an animal shelter
- ◯ Take photos of each other
- ◯ Try local transportation
- ◯ Make a time capsule
- ◯ Take a yoga class together

- ◯ Close your eyes and draw each other
- ◯ Bake a cake together
- ◯ Meditate together
- ◯ Get a psychic reading together
- ◯ Wash your cars together

SOURCES AND RESOURCES

MANY OF THESE fifty-two tips are adaptations of those that first appeared in the blog section of the website Craig Lambert Couples Therapy (craiglamberttherapy.com). Please visit the website for many more tips and resources.

In the book, we have mentioned several concepts that Craig learned when, many years ago, he and his late wife took some workshops with Harville Hendrix and Helen LaKelly Hunt. Later on, Craig decided to become certified in Imago relationship therapy, which was created by Harville and Helen. Craig was certified in this technique, in Pasadena, by Bruce and Francine Creppishette. The processes in tips 3, 11, 13, and 15 draw on material from this training with Harville and Helen and the Creppishettes, as do the mirroring, validation, empathy, and deconstructing anger exercises. The processes are also discussed and taught in several books by Harville and Helen, including those listed below. The quote from Harville in tip 27 was gleaned from a workshop.

Aron, Arthur, Edward Melinat, Elaine N. Aron, Robert Darrin Vallone, and Renee J. Bator. "The Experimental Generation of Interpersonal Closeness: A Procedure and Some Preliminary Findings." *Personality and Social Psychology Bulletin* 23, no. 4 (April 1997): 363–77. https://journals.sagepub.com/doi/pdf/10.1177/0146167297234003.

Benson, Kyle. "The Magic Relationship Ratio, According to Science." *The Gottman Relationship Blog*, October 4, 2017. https://www.gottman.com/blog/the-magic-relationship-ratio-according-science/.

Ben-Zeév, Aaron. "Why a Lover's Touch Is So Powerful." *Psychology Today*, May 18, 2014. https://www.psychologytoday.com/ca/blog/in-the-name-love/201405/why-lovers-touch-is-so-powerful.

Brittle, Zach. "R Is for Repair." *The Gottman Relationship Blog*, September 3, 2014. https://www.gottman.com/blog/r-is-for-repair/.

Brittle, Zach. "Turn Towards Instead of Away." *The Gottman Relationship Blog*, April 1, 2015. https://www.gottman.com/blog/turn-toward-instead-of-away/.

Catron, Mandy Len. "To Fall in Love with Anyone, Do This." *New York Times*, January 9, 2015. https://www.nytimes.com/2015/01/11/fashion/modern-love-to-fall-in-love-with-anyone-do-this.html.

Chapman, Gary. *The 5 Love Languages: The Secret to Love That Lasts*. Chicago: Northfield Publishing, 1992.

His Holiness the Dalai Lama, and Howard C. Cutler. *The Art of Happiness: A Handbook for Living* (10th Anniversary Edition). New York: Riverhead Books, 2009.

Gottman, John. *The Seven Principles for Making Marriage Work: A Practical Guide from the Country's Foremost Relationship Expert*. New York: Harmony Books, 1999, 2015.

Headley, Jason, dir. "It's Not About the Nail." http://jasonheadley.com/INATN.html or https://www.youtube.com/watch?v=-4EDhdAHrOg.

Hendrix, Harville. *Getting the Love You Want: A Guide for Couples*. New York: Harper Perennial, 1990.

Hendrix, Harville, and Helen LaKelly Hunt. *Making Marriage Simple: Ten Relationship-Saving Truths*. New York: Harmony Books, 2014.

Hendrix, Harville, and Helen LaKelly Hunt. *The Personal Companion: Meditations and Exercises for Keeping the Love You Find*. New York: Simon & Schuster, 1995.

McDaniel, Brandon, and Sarah Coyne. "'Technoference': The Interference of Technology in Couple Relationships and Implications for Women's Personal and Relational Well-Being." *Psychology of Popular Media Culture* 5, no. 1 (2016): 85–98. http://dx.doi.org/10.1037/ppm0000065.

Moore, Tracy. "Scheduling Sex Could Save Your Relationship —But There's a Right and Wrong Way to Do It." *MEL*. https://melmagazine.com/en-us/story/scheduling-sex-could-save-your-relationship-but-theres-a-right-and-wrong-way-to-do-it.

Nietzsche, Friedrich. *The Will to Power*. Translated by Walter Kaufmann and R. J. Hollingdale. New York: Random House, 1967.

Real, Terrence. *The New Rules of Marriage: What You Need to Know to Make Love Work*. New York: Ballantine Books, 2007.

The RSA. "Brené Brown on Empathy." Katie Davis, animation. YouTube, December 10, 2013. https://www.youtube.com/watch?v=1Evwgu369Jw.

SoulPancake. "How to Connect with Anyone." February 12, 2015. https://www.youtube.com/watch?v=Xm-T3HCa618&t=1s.

Ury, Logan. "Want to Improve Your Relationship? Start Paying More Attention to Bids." *The Gottman Relationship Blog*, February 11, 2019. https://www.gottman.com/blog/want-to-improve-your-relationship-start-paying-more-attention-to-bids/.

Williamson, Marianne. *A Return to Love: Reflections on the Principles of a Course in Miracles*. New York: HarperCollins, 1993.

FURTHER READINGS AND VIEWINGS

As with the works cited above, these reading and viewing suggestions have very practical information for therapists and couples alike. Couples who keep the learning going are generally happier and more successful resolving conflicts. Think of a relationship as playing an instrument or a sport: the learning never stops, and as knowledge grows, so does joy and satisfaction. We hope you enjoy these resources as much as we do!

As/Is. "Weird Things All Couples Fight About." YouTube, September 6, 2014. https://www.youtube.com/watch?v=Fi07T6mjCbI&Feature=youtu.be.

Corn, Laura. *101 Nights of Grrreat Romance: Secret Sealed Seductions for Fun-Loving Couples*. New York: Park Avenue, 1996.

Godek, Gregory J.P. *1001 Ways to Be Romantic: More Romantic Than Ever*. Naperville, IL: Sourcebooks Casablanca, 2010.

McCarthy Miller, Beth, dir. *Modern Family*. Season 2, episode 17, "Two Monkeys and a Panda." Aired on March 2, 2011.

Oprah's SuperSoul Conversations. "Dr. Brené Brown: The Ana tomy of Trust." YouTube, July 14, 2019. https://youtu.be/HX7pxiwzSzQ.

Perel, Esther. *Mating in Captivity: Reconciling the Erotic and the Domestic*. New York: HarperCollins, 2006.

ACCESS A GOTTMAN Institute Repair-Attempts Questionnaire, which we recommend for the practice in tip 32, in the following article:

Fulwiler, Michael. "Weekend Homework Assignment: Repair Attempts." *The Gottman Relationship Blog*, September 5, 2014. https://www.gottman.com/blog/weekend-homework-assignment-repair-attempts-2/.

THE FOLLOWING APPS are those we recommend for the practice in tip 39. Download one or all of them and enjoy!

36 Questions: http://36questionsinlove.com/
Couple Game: https://couplegame.app/
Gottman Card Decks: https://www.gottman.com/couples/apps/
Pillow: https://pillow.io/. (Note: the Pillow app is no longer available but the content is still downloadable at this link for a small fee.)

YOU CAN ALSO find the list of Aron's 36 questions here:

Jones, Daniel. "The 36 Questions That Lead to Love." *New York Times*, January 9, 2015. https://www.nytimes.com/2015/01/11/fashion/no-37-big-wedding-or-small.html.

EPIGRAPHS

Many of the epigraphs are quotes from online sources such as goodreads.com, brainyquote.com, and azquotes.com. Others are from the following sources:

TIP 7

Saladino, Lynn. Quoted in Salaky, Kristin. "How to Talk to Your Partner About Their Weight and Body Image." *Insider*, August 31, 2017. https://www.insider.com/how-do-you-talk-to-your-partner-about-body-weight-2017-8.

TIPS 9 AND 12

Gibran, Kahlil. *The Prophet.* New York: Alfred A. Knopf, 1923.

TIP 10

Chapman, Gary. "Discover Your Spouse's Love Language." *Focus on the Family.* https://www.focusonthefamily.com/marriage/discovering-your-spouses-love-language/.

TIP 15

Hendrix, Harville. *Getting the Love That You Want*, 1990.

TIP 24

Quoted in "Scientists Explain 5 Ways Technology Can Hurt Your Relationship." *Power of Positivity.* https://www.powerofpositivity.com/technology-hurt-relationship/.

TIP 27

Rumi, Jalal al-Din. *The Essential Rumi.* Coleman Barks, trans., with John Moyne. New York: HarperCollins, 1995.

TIP 32

Dreyfus, Nancy. *Talk to Me Like I'm Someone You Love: Relationship Repair in a Flash.* New York: Tarcher/Penguin, 1993.

TIPS 39 AND 41

Perel, Esther. *Mating in Captivity: Reconciling the Erotic and the Domestic*. New York: HarperCollins, 2006.

TIP 42

This epigraph is a paraphrased version of comments Terrence Real made during a webinar Craig attended. Please see Terrence Real's website for resources: https://www.terryreal.com.

TIP 44

Hesse, Hermann. *Siddhartha.* New York: Bantam Books, 1971.

TIP 47

Savage, Dan. "Savage Love: Buzz Kill." *The Stranger*, January 22, 2009. https://www.thestranger.com/seattle/SavageLove?oid=999857.

TIP 51

Perel, Esther. Quoted in Kornbluth, Jesse. "*Mating in Captivity*: Esther Perel Reconciles 'Sex' and 'Marriage.'" Interview with Esther Perel. *Life Blog*, November 17, 2011. https://www.huffpost.com/entry/mating-in-captivity-esthe_n_70481.

ABOUT THE AUTHORS

CRAIG LAMBERT AND DEBBIE LAMBERT are relationship experts, each with more than thirty years of experience in the areas of communication and relationships. With a focus on strengthening relationships and improving communication, Craig and Debbie help frustrated, hurting couples gain new understanding of themselves, their partners, and even the world around them.

Craig Lambert, LCSW, is dedicated to helping couples rekindle their love, deepen their intimacy, and strengthen their communication. He has worked with hundreds of San Diego couples, helping them understand the often unconscious underpinnings of relationship conflict.

Debbie Lambert is a relationship educator and coach with a special talent for helping couples repair and build healthier relationships. She is also a life coach and pioneer in the field of personal transformation. Debbie is a bestselling author, is not sure about this creator of the Ladder of Life, and has written numerous articles in the area of psychology, personal development, and the mind/spirit/body connection. Debbie is currently working on a book about how to use the Ladder of Life to emerge from the muck of our lives.

Visit craiglamberttherapy.com for more information.

Printed in Great Britain
by Amazon

82839119R00150